*Living and
Growing Together*

Living and Growing Together

Today's Christian Family

GARY COLLINS, editor

WORD BOOKS, Publisher • Waco, Texas

Contents

THE FAMILY AND OUTSIDE PRESSURES

THE FAMILY REACHING OUT

Introduction

Several years ago a number of family life experts were surveyed and asked to list the greatest changes that they had observed in families during recent times. The increasing divorce rate (now over 1 million annually in the U.S.) was most frequently mentioned. Then came the decreasing influence of the husband and father in the home, the increase in sexual intercourse apart from marriage, the growing number of working wives, and the decline in family size. Add to this such things as widespread confusion over male and female roles, the constant mobility in our society which keeps families on the move and far away from relatives, the hectic life-style and excessive busyness of family members with all of their activities outside of the home, and it is easy to understand why many people wonder if the family can or even should survive.

In the lives of many people, it would appear that the home is becoming less and less important. There are numerous demands on our time from outside the family, so much so that for many people the home is little more than a convenient place to sleep, grab a bite to eat, and get the laundry done. This, of course, affects every member of the family. The father too often is absent or, when he does come home, too tired to get involved in family activities. The mother is either working to supplement the family income or involved in activities which are, for many, more fulfilling than homemaking. The children, including teenagers, are either left alone or caught up in their own round of community, school, and other activities.

Even the church has been blamed for hindering family unity. With frequent meetings, programs geared to different age groups, men's fellowships and women's circles, children's clubs and teen activities, committed Christians sometimes find that their place of worship keeps them so busy that there is no time for family togetherness. And even when there is time to be together many people aren't sure what they could be doing to build unity or to have fun as a family.

Each of the writers of this book has given serious consideration to family problems such as these and in the following pages each offers practical help for Christian families who are living and growing together. At the Continental Congress on the Family, held recently in St. Louis, each of these chapters was presented verbally, debated enthusiastically and revised subsequently for inclusion in this book.

Edith Schaeffer, popular author and Christian homemaker from L'Abri in Switzerland, begins the book with her definition of what a family really is. This is followed by five chapters dealing with the internal aspects of family togetherness: family emotional maturity (Hyder), parenthood (Narramore), the challenge of teenagers (Kessler), family finances (Werning) and vacations (Gwinn).

Sometimes family unity is strained or shattered by pressures that come from outside the home and are beyond the control of family members. Senator Mark Hatfield discusses some of these pressures in his chapter which, incidentally, was the opening address at the Continental Congress on the Family. Ted Ward continues the same theme with a chapter on the family and society which brought forth some of the most positive reactions from Congress participants. Psychiatrists Basel Jackson and Markham Berry then follow with chapters, respectively, on teen-age drug use, and the effects on a family when one of its members is mentally or physically ill.

The book concludes with two chapters on ways by which families can reach out to the world around. Matthew Prince describes what he calls friendship evangelism, and Leighton Ford's chapter (which was the closing Congress address) gives a challenge for all Christian families to be involved in spreading the gospel through the family unit.

J. Allan Petersen, president of Family Concern, Omaha, Nebraska, first conceived the idea of a Continental Congress on the Family. He mobilized the resources and directed the many details which brought the Congress, and subsequent books, into existence. It was his hope that the Congress would alert Christians in North America and abroad to the needs of the family and would stimulate all of us to build better families in our communities and churches, but especially in our homes. The North American family has a long way to go before its problems are solved. Hopefully this book will take many families at least one step further in the direction of greater and more widespread family stability.

GARY R. COLLINS

1.

What Is a Family?

Edith Schaeffer

There seems to be confusion today as to what a family is. The word *family* has been stretched and pulled out of context until it has ceased to mean anything at all to some people. One human being committed to another human being in some way does not make a family. A church, a commune, single people sharing a house, or people committed to other people do not make what is basically meant by the term *family*. It is good to broaden the word to speak of the "church family," the "neighborhood family," or the "camp family" in referring to the warm, close relationship of the larger group, but all these broader meanings have no reality without a well-defined basic meaning.

Essentially, the *family* consists of a man and a woman who are married to each other and the children they have borne, and this is a biblical definition. The Scripture calls children a heritage of the Lord (Ps. 127) and describes the familial structure in vivid terms: "Thy wife shall be as a fruitful vine by the sides of thine house: thy children like olive plants round about thy table" (Ps. 128:3). The admonitions of the Word of God to parents are in relationship to their responsibilities to those born of their own bodies, and this basic structure must not be blurred by widening

---

Edith Schaeffer, along with her husband Dr. Francis Schaeffer, founded L'Abri, the world-famous Christian community in Switzerland. She is the author of several books, including *L'Abri* and *Hidden Art*.

the meaning of the word *family*. This framework continues generation after generation in the relationship of children with grandparents and great-grandparents from whom they have descended.

Everyone has been born of a mother and begotten by a father; however, not everyone has been nurtured by both parents or even by one natural parent. Nevertheless, this fact does not change the basic meaning of the word *family*. Unfortunately, some people are very alone because this is a fallen world and things are abnormal. But solitary individuals are not helped by attempts to redefine the family. God says that when we become his children we become members of the wider family, and since he is our Father, we are "adopted" by compassionate human beings who are also his children.

God created the family, making first the man and then the woman and giving them reproductive capabilities. In God's plan they would together bring forth a human being who would be part of each of them, but the Fall occurred before the first baby was born, and no baby has ever been born into a perfect atmosphere. Therefore, it takes imagination, commitment, hard work, love, and time to become what a family is meant to be.

How much time? It seems to me, a lifetime is needed, for a family is a complex blending of relationships, personalities, minds, and emotions, a living mobile of changing human beings. You have seen mobiles—slim wood shapes or fine blown glass strung on invisible threads, moving with every breath of air. A family is an ever-changing blend of people, never two days the same in age or development, strung together by threads of history and experience. A family is a work of art that needs long years of tending and must often be repaired. When Rembrandt's *Night Watch* was senselessly slashed, the first reaction of the Dutch museum authorities was to plan its painstaking repair. Junking the masterpiece was never considered. A family is a precious, valuable work of art. When it is torn or vandalized, the talents of an expert are available for its repair—the Father.

A family is an ecologically balanced environment for the growth of human beings. Ecologists are worried about imbalances in nature. Oxygen is being diminished because algae are destroyed in the oceans; bugs are attacking crops because certain birds have been destroyed. But the most essential environment for the development of human personalities is the family. Each mother and father make a unique contribution to his or her children. Together they give the caring that is a human necessity, and as in all human relationships, balance is important. In the family blended balance is vital if children are to perceive mothers and fathers as extensions of God the Father and his love. Especially is this true in nurturing dependence and independence.

Recently I talked to a young man who said his parents taught him to be independent in such harsh ways that he feels he never experienced tenderness and compassion from them. For instance, when he was ten years old, he fell and seriously cut his leg. His mother said, "Call the hospital, get yourself a taxi, and go get it sewn up." Now he accomplished what was supposed to make a man of him. However, he can never go back and have what he missed, someone to lovingly go with him at ten, tell him stories to make him forget the pain, hold his hand, and show compassion and true sympathy.

Dependence is often thought of as a bad thing; yet, in the right balance, dependence is good. Feeling that one can always trust and depend on mother and dad helps a person know what trusting and depending on God means as well as how to treat human beings. God's Word speaks of two being better than one; when one falls, the other can pick him up.

The knowledge that there are people who care about us in a warm, personal way often protects us from doing extreme or foolish things during times of sudden stress and encourages us to keep going when things seem hopeless or desperate.

A family is a shelter in the time of storm. This is a picture of what God is to his family: "Hear my cry, O God . . . For thou hast been a shelter for me, and a strong tower from the enemy" (Ps. 61:1, 3). If our earthly family is really a shelter, we can help our children understand the faithfulness of God. The storms of illness, psychological upset, crippling disease, handicaps, old age, death, or accident can be weathered in the shelter of the family.

Sickness and hurts, whether physical or psychological, need proper loving care. I find great ignorance as to what constitutes loving, kind, good care. One needs to know when one is neglecting to give the best care to sick children, distressed adults, or elderly people. "Doing it unto the Lord by doing it unto the least of these" should be a reality first in the family.

The storms of bankruptcy, fire, polio, hayfever, cancer, or broken legs are not interruptions of family life but a part of it. Weathering storms together draws family members closer to one another. Helping during difficult times rather than splitting apart cements emotional ties and becomes a shared experience that represents love and concern. Such an atmosphere provides shelter from outside persecution as well as from illness and pain.

A family is an economic unit. God gave Adam and Eve the possibility of leading a perfect existence—with creative work as a source of joy. Their only restriction was not to eat the fruit of a certain tree. They chose to believe Satan's lies rather than God's word verbalized to them, and they ate of the tree. Part of their punishment was that they would have to work in order to eat. God said to Adam, "In the sweat of thy face shalt thou eat bread, till thou return unto the ground" (Gen. 3:19). To this day people must work to provide the necessities of life although through inventions and discoveries God has allowed people to ease their work load.

"In sickness and in health, for richer or for poorer" is more than a marriage vow; it is a statement about family life. The ups and downs are to be shared. The work involved in providing for a family needs to be shared, and this is a matter quite apart from whether or not a woman should work outside the home.

It has always seemed rather ridiculous to me to designate going to an office as "work" and to designate the rich variety of activities and responsibilities involved in caring full time for a family as "not work, just housekeeping." To pretend that the family member who has a cash salary is the only one providing material things is to be totally blind to the one providing the balance to that contribution by cooking, nursing sick children, interior decorating, planting gardens, preparing times to read aloud for fun or education, sewing, driving the family "taxi," and so on. I contend that every homemaker *earns* a very large portion of the total it takes to live. The family as an economic unit is not a matter of dollars and cents but a matter of having the greatest freedom to produce that which is needed and appreciated.

There is, however, no complete democracy, and in the family there must be a "head." Christ, the bridegroom, is the head of his bride, the church; but the bridegroom serves (as Christ demonstrated by washing the disciples' feet), and the bridegroom gives responsibilities to the bride (as Christ has given the responsibilities of making truth known to the church).

But because there is an "order" in the home, this does not mean that there are men's jobs and women's jobs. There is no reason a man cannot be a fine chef; therefore there is no reason a man cannot cook the turkey as well as carve it. There is no reason a man should not design and make clothing, nor is there any reason a man should not be the interior decorator in his own home as well as in his business. Talents differ; people differ. No two people are alike, and no two couples are alike. It is wrong to lay down rules as to exact details. A mother and a father should share in caring for the children—reading to them, bathing them. However, just as there needs to be a "head" of the home, there needs to be a homemaker who blends all that the home needs, making the job close to what it should be—a full career.

I do think homemaking should be the wife's career, and additional talents should be fulfilled "around the edges" as the virtuous woman did in Proverbs 31. This passage makes it clear that a good wife has much freedom to do a great variety of creative things. This woman didn't sit in a corner doing nothing; she wasn't a nonperson. She bought a field and landscaped it for a vineyard. She wove cloth from linen she had grown and made clothing for her family plus some to sell. She not only imported spices and rare foods but sold things in the marketplace. She also cared for the poor. However, all her work helped her husband to be known at the gates. She enhanced his place among others; she did not compete with it.

I feel a mother can do any kind of work she is capable of if she really puts her home first and considers her home a career and a work of art. It takes time to make the home all that a family needs. The woman in Proverbs 31 had time to be a good wife and mother; her husband praised her, and her children rose up and called her blessed. She didn't neglect the things of the Lord, because she is described as one really close to the Lord. She spoke with wisdom, and kindness was in her tongue.

The woman in Proverbs was skillful, energetic, and capable; yet she did not neglect her home. To consider an office job glamorous and home a bore is a limited view indeed of the possibilities in homemaking. But certainly there is nothing wrong with a "working woman" or a "working mother" if she does not neglect the next generation entrusted to her care or neglect her career as homemaker and wife.

The balance between affluence and poverty is a matter between individuals and God. But the "togetherness" of the family must not be put aside for affluence; the balance must be carefully maintained. Life goes by too quickly and cannot be lived twice. A child either has a warm, loving, imaginative home full of the mother's creativity, or he or she grows up in emptiness. We must ask, At what price are there two "going out to work" parents during the children's growing-up years?

As finite human beings, we must balance the use of time because we can only do one thing at a time. Each month, each year children and parents grow and change. New interests and new understandings should give variety and provide fresh starts for the whole family. A family is never static, and the order of male and female does not dictate a ledger marking off regulated activities. Even if the father follows the same career task all his life and the mother makes home and family her single career, the possibilities for assuming new and creative roles are endless.

A family is a creativity center. Artists, sculptors, scientists, engineers, inventors, musicians, painters, poets, writers, cooks, designers of gardens or dresses or book jackets—human beings—need fertile ground in which to grow. Not only should children feel free to start creative projects, but husbands and wives should encourage each other. The home should be a rich source of inspiration for all kinds of creativity—taking violin lessons, learning to make Japanese flower arrangements, starting to grow bean sprouts for a Chinese dinner six days later, writing a play and putting it on in the living room.

Creative talent should be nourished, not squashed with loud laughter or teasing or crushed by putting the wrong things first. Creativity needs appreciation, affirmation from another person. Criticism should never be given at the important moment—the unveiling of the completed project. Anything said at that moment must be positive. The right response at the right time is essential to encourage the next stage of creative endeavor. Instead of chasing a three-year-old out of the kitchen, help him or her cut carrots, "make" cookies, break an egg into a bowl. Of course, a budding chef complicates the scene, but twenty years later a son will feel no hesitation about preparing a good Italian spaghetti dinner for his family or friends. The results are worth the trouble and the mess when creative impulses bud and blossom.

The Bible does *not* rule out creativity as a spiritual experience. The instructions for the tabernacle, given to Moses in the Book of Exodus, included fantastic works of art. Obviously, people needed creative skills to produce these things. This artwork had beauty as well as spiritual meaning. God's house was meant to be beautiful. The works of art were made in family groups, and skills were developed in a home atmosphere in ancient times.

A family is a perpetual relay of truth. God makes it very clear in his Word, in Deuteronomy as well as in many other places, that children are to hear the truth from their parents. Truth about God was meant to be given to children by parents and grandparents: "Tell your sons and your sons' sons . . ." "And when your son asks . . ." True answers are to be given. Truth would not have been lost had it been handed down at the breakfast table, at lunch, at dinner, at bedtime, when out walking together, or when sitting together before a sunset or a fire. To the family God handed the responsibility for passing on to the generations of the earth knowledge about him, about what had happened in past history, and about how to worship him now.

Fathers and mothers have been cruel to their children in neglecting to make truth known and in neglecting to make it exciting. Cain not only killed Abel; Cain turned his own children away from the knowledge of coming to God with a lamb by refusing to come himself. The excitement and the reality of all the Bible teaches should be a normal part of discussion; the Bible and other books should be read aloud together in the family. The reality of the family's dependence upon God in prayer for guidance and his care cannot be supplied by the church. It must be lived day by day as the family prays together concerning a crisis, problems, or trivial incidents. Doubts must be discussed calmly but seriously, even with a five-year-old.

A preschool child may ask, "Who made the devil?" and be dealing with the whole problem of evil. The answer should be a positive, truthful explanation. Discussion should not be delayed until a child is some particular "age." It must take place when the need for information surfaces and must continue when illustrations present themselves. Relaying truth takes time and imagination, and doing it properly involves treating a child of any age as a human being with value and importance.

Children are people, personalities, individuals. No two are alike, and each must be treated as a unique person from the very beginning. When a child is two years old, he or she will demonstrate traits that portend the twenty-two-year-old. The friend you make of your three-year-old will be your closest friend and joy when he or she is thirty-three. Children are not objects to discipline who later become adults to get to know. They are people from the start with memories and personalities. Children who become your friends and who love to talk with you when they are tiny never stop loving to talk to you and to bring you their thoughts and ideas as they grow older. Initiate trust, deep confidence, and love at the earliest moments, even before replies can be made to you in words. It can easily be too late, but it can never be too early. A three-year-old can ask questions which will lead to discussion and understanding that will last a lifetime.

A family is a museum of memories. Memories can "happen," but memories can also be planned. A schedule is splendid, but on occasions seeing a full moon rise over the sea or over a mountain or through a tree is more important than making a child go to bed on time. When figuring the cost of certain things, the reality that you are "buying a memory" should be taken into account. The memory of a symphony concert enjoyed as a family, the warmth of sharing favorite moments of the music in conversation afterward, stopping for a hot chocolate on the way home, or having a flower in one's hair for the evening can be a help years later in crucial moments of sudden decision.

Memories should be "collected" for the family with some amount of attention. Taking a picnic to the park or stopping at the zoo on the way home from marketing may legitimately take priority over getting a piece of work accomplished. In light of what kind of memories are being collected, what constitutes "wasted time" might frequently be reconsidered. To make a "memory" of a boringly long night-drive by reading an interesting story aloud by flashlight is worth all the cricks one gets in the neck. Memories of Christmas, birthdays, and the first day of school should be warm and special because mother or father or an older sister or brother was imaginative and thoughtful. But gentle, loving compassion should be expressed in a great diversity of ways that will make many days which have no calendar significance into private warm memories.

Of course there will also be memories of frustrations and family arguments. These will not necessarily harm any family member, and they help children to learn that people have good and bad moods and that people make mistakes. Parents need to reassure children, however, that bad times do not mean the home is falling apart. Facing the fact that the members of one's family have faults and weaknesses prepares a child for relationships outside the family by helping him or her to understand that no one is perfect.

There are no perfect people, no perfect marriages, and no perfect relationships. And therefore mothers and fathers and children need not feel guilty about not being the perfectly ideal family. We all make a mess of it at times and need to make new starts. Forgiveness is an important aspect of family life. Since no parent is perfect, he or she cannot be perfect in forgiveness, but forgiveness is a two-sided coin and should be learned in childhood. Parents need to forgive each other and their children, and they also need to ask forgiveness of their children.

Sensitivity to another's needs and feelings, sympathy, understanding, compassion, and forgiveness are taught by example. Children observe disagreements between parents; they should also witness apologies and forgiveness.

Parents show something of the way God treats us as his children in the way they treat their own children. How can a child comprehend God's love and forgiveness unless he or she has experienced with wonderful certainty the complete forgiveness of a parent? As a child builds a museum of family memories, the words *father* and *mother* should conjure up a flood of understanding.

A family is an educational control. Here the word *control* is used in the French sense of a monitoring system. Parents should keep a careful watch over what is taking place in the developing education of each child. Schools can help or hinder, and an informed parent can create a necessary balance in a child's home environment to counteract or support the school's influence. For example, if the classroom seems too rigid, a child can be urged toward creative freedom at home. If the school is too free and there seems to be a lack of mental discipline, parents can structure household tasks to be accomplished in a certain amount of time, suggest poems to be memorized, or devise mental arithmetic games. The home should be the most educationally stimulating experience in a child's background.

Parents need to show children the connection between their education and their Christian faith. The two cannot be separated, for God is God of the whole person. Open discussion and communication at home is vital. Encourage your children to read by reading aloud with them, perhaps at set times each week. Include a wide variety of subject matter—music, gardening, fishing and sports, sex, childbirth, abortion, drugs. Children need to feel free to question, and parents need to feel free to say, "I don't know, but I'll try to find out." God will provide guidance and wisdom to those who seek him, and a child can be encouraged to ask God directly for his answers and his day-by-day plan.

Education in life and education in the Word of God should never be compartmentalized. The family can nurture trust and belief in the existence of answers for those who believe in a personal universe created by a personal God.

A family is a formation center for human relationships. Tiny children can learn that people are more important than things, that human beings are made in the image of God and are therefore very special. How to treat people is not a subject to be lectured about; it should be taught in the middle of real life situations within the family.

A child, propelled on feet sloshing along in muddy shoes, rushes into mother with a clump of wild flowers and weeds clutched tightly in a hot little hand. What is the response? "Get that mud out of this room! How many times have I told you . . ." Or, "What a lovely bunch of flowers! I'll get a vase and water, and we'll put them on the kitchen table." Mother plants a kiss on a child glowing in the aftermath of affirmation. Then, "Honey, remember to get the mud off your shoes outside first. Try not to forget, will you?"

The scream, "Get out of here," crushes and debilitates as it teaches a vivid lesson in how to treat other people and the relative value of persons and things. Human relationships on all levels are derived from essential childhood experiences.

Expressions of love are an important ingredient in human relationships, and the family circle provides daily opportunities to demonstrate love in action. Love is not just a feeling; love is a choice. One chooses to love another person, and the choice must be made over and over again, day by day. Feeling is not the criterion for love. Love is a matter of reason, intellect, and decision. It is not enhanced by magnifying another's faults but by dwelling on the lovely qualities and kindnesses and thoughtful attempts to please.

Love for one another and love for the Lord grow when we nourish them. The feelings and emotions of love are a result of daily choices. Love doesn't hit like lightning and last forever; it grows with time and care. Seeds planted in lush soil still need sunshine, water, fertilizer, and weeding to grow into healthy plants free of snails and bugs.

Time is an essential ingredient in growing loving family relationships. This means that if the Lord is first in a family the family members will put their relationships first at times because the Lord means for the family to be together.

A family is an open door—with hinges and a lock. The Bible clearly commands Christian families to be hospitable. "Use hospitality one to another without grudging" (1 Pet. 4:9). "Be not forgetful to entertain strangers: for thereby some have entertained angels unawares" (Heb. 13:2).

Families are to share their life with strangers, people in need, the elderly, the lonely, the lost, the handicapped, but it is impossible to share what one does not have. At specific times the door needs to swing shut—a portion of every day, maybe at bedtime; a day off just for the family to be together; vacations. Sometimes privacy is essential if only to argue.

When the door swings open, Christian families can share their resources with a society greatly endangered by the breakdown in family life. To show hospitality is a biblical admonition, but the extent of the hospitality needs the Lord's leading. The important thing is that we teach and live the gospel, the truth. When we share with others, we are really sharing with the Lord, but we must ask the Lord to send no more at a time than we are able to care for—as human beings, not evangelistic objects.

It would be difficult to isolate the most important characteristic of the family, but surely the idea of continuity is one of the primary considerations. Human beings need life-continuity. Unfortunately, the search for personal happiness, personal fulfillment, and personal rights often obliterates the reality of these goals and shreds life into torn bits and pieces.

Individuals need the comfort and security found in continuous relationship with preceding and succeeding generations. Continuity of the generations provides a wider closeness than is possible within the nuclear family. Grandparents are important; children need to know old people. They can also gain perspective from single aunts and uncles. Widows need brothers and uncles and brothers-in-law to help with their fatherless sons. Middle-aged people need to belong to young people and old people.

God's given formula is to "die" if you want to live. To die to self and selfishness and to consider the needs of others, first within the family and then within a wider circle, is what Jesus meant when he said, "He that loseth his life shall find it." To say, "Love thy family" is to say, "Be longsuffering," and that takes years and years of diverse sacrifices. It is also to say, "Be kind," and that takes imagination and work. We are told that love bears all things, endures all things, and never fails. How long does it take practically to live out such love? How much continuity? A lifetime.

Inside the Family

2.

Developing Family Emotional Maturity

Quentin Hyder

There is no such unit as a *normal* family for the reason that there is no such being as a *normal* person. Everyone has some minor neurotic tendencies or at least some minor interpersonal relationship problems that cause him occasionally to relate to people in other than harmonious ways. Only Jesus Christ was completely normal in the sense of perfect. I therefore tend to think not so much of *normal* as being our goal, but rather *ideal*. Ideal does not mean perfect but does imply hope in some higher standard. To strive for an ideal family gives us a goal to shoot for which is realistically attainable and recognizes the imperfections of human failure. These failures tend to keep us humble and forgiving toward one another.

One thinks generally of a family as consisting of children and their two parents, but we must remember that there are many variations. These include single-parent families, remarriage situations with two or three groups of children having different combinations of natural parents, families with a permanently domiciled grandparent or other peripheral member, and the sometimes significant problem of either occasional or frequent intervention by in-laws.

Quentin Hyder, M.D., practices psychiatry in New York City and is involved in clinical research in depression at the Columbia Presbyterian Medical Center. He is the medical director of the Christian Counseling and Psychotherapy Center in midtown Manhattan and also serves on the faculty of the New York School of the Bible.

The foundations for stability and maturity in an ideal family necessarily stem from the relationship of the husband and wife with each other. The two outstanding basic causes of marital disharmony from which all other specific problems in the family ultimately derive are thoughtlessness and selfishness. Thoughtlessness in its extreme is foolishness which is a psychological or emotional problem. Selfishness is a sin which is a spiritual problem. Both can be worked out among family members who desire to communicate with humility and who exhibit a willingness to respect opinions contrary to their own. Unless both genuine communication and mutual respect are present in a relationship, even professional counseling will be of little avail.

Love is the essential ingredient which maintains communication and respect. Without it the relationship is lifeless. Many couples who come to see me no longer love each other. I help them to understand each other better, to communicate better, and to work out some compromise for their differences. I cannot restore lost love, but Christian couples who believe that God is the giver of life and love should pray that God, who gave them their love for each other in the first place, will rekindle it and thereby revive their relationship. If both sincerely desire it, God can show them new, creative ways to express their love and sustain it in spite of conflicts.

Stability and maturity in a home can be developed and maintained if all family members recognize a few basic principles.

Love must be outwardly expressed, not only constantly toward the children, but also between the parents in front of the children. One of the greatest factors in the development of a child's emotional security is seeing his parents hold hands, kiss and hug, and in many ways show their affection and love for each other. During each day parents of small children should frequently hold them close, talk with them at their level, and play with them, either with their toys or by simply romping on the floor. Parents must not allow their own worries and problems to become barriers to love. Christian parents should ask God to give them sustaining love for their children, especially when children are disobedient or behave in an unlovable way. Love should be demonstrated by attention and by verbal expressions of affection. Children who are loved, who know they are loved, who grow up in a home in which this is an unchanging reality for them and for their parents, will grow into secure, emotionally mature adolescents and adults. They will be able to relate to others with self-assurance and confidence and will one day be able to provide homes in which their own children can also grow up to be emotionally stable and personally secure.

Inadequate attention and a lack of demonstrative love can cause a child to feel unwanted or unappreciated. If love and approval are not securely available at home, a child may seek to fulfill these needs elsewhere, risking frustration, rejection, or some other form of emotional pain.

Parents who not only deeply love their children but frequently demonstrate that love by word and action will enable them to develop through adolescence to adulthood secure in the fact they are wanted and appreciated. The emotional security of a loving home is the greatest single factor in obviating a child's need to search for satisfaction in superficial and ultimately disappointing relationships outside.

Giving is one of the cardinal manifestations of love. Giving is not just buying Christmas and birthday presents. Giving means involvement, spending time, caring, teaching, being interested, sharing, empathizing, and above all, being willing to sacrifice one's own desires when in conflict with those of others.

Mature individuals and mature families possess the ability to postpone gratification. The decision to put off until a more appropriate time the satisfaction of a desire, such as for a particular vacation trip or a new family station wagon, will strengthen the bonds of family unity. Further, any mutually endured hardship or suffering deepens the sense of comradeship among all family members. This in turn develops a unifying purpose and a clear sense of being members of a team that is working together to achieve harmony in the home.

Understanding and respect for individual differences are essential to family stability. Most groups of people living together have widely differing personal characteristics. Recognizing one's own and others' temperamental types and personality structures and adapting to the differences are vital to the creation of mature relationships.

Financial difficulties leading to disharmony can almost always be straightened out in a family conference if all are willing to yield personal ambitions to the security of the home. The following principles should be discussed and agreed upon by all concerned:

1. Carefully calculate and create a family budget.
2. Appropriately assign various purchasing and debt-paying responsibilities.
3. Build a reserve savings account and eventually, if possible, an investment portfolio.
4. Arrange adequate insurance coverage on life, health, and property.
5. Agree to commit a minimum percentage of income in the form of tithes and offerings to the work of the Lord.

Good communication leads to joyful communion. The words *communication* and *communion* have a common Latin root, the meaning of which embraces the ideal of togetherness. Successful communication among family members requires mutual understanding of, not only verbalized meaning, but also concomitant emotion, whether outwardly expressed or not. True empathy has been described as "your pain in my heart." Family communication and communion cause pain at times, but peace and satisfaction come when differences are resolved. Peace must not be attained at any price, however, especially if the price is bottled up in unexpressed anger or resentment. As God is in the light, we are exhorted to walk in the light, and this might mean openly sharing inner thoughts which disturb family harmony.

Good communication is not complete until three stages have been achieved: (1) the giver imparts the message either verbally or nonverbally; (2) the receiver fully understands the message; (3) the receiver responds appropriately to the message (either agreement or disagreement), and the giver understands that response. In order to accomplish this, all participants must be honest, trustful, sincere in desiring to understand the others' viewpoints, and willing to yield their own cravings to the greater cause of family good. Successful communication involves one essential prerequisite for Christians. All must sincerely want to know and to do God's will. If they desire this, God will step in and help them toward mutual understanding, respect, and love.

Achieving this, however, takes time in prayer, humbly listening to the Lord to ascertain his will, imparted to the mind by the Holy Spirit. Listen prayerfully also to other members of the body of Christ and concerned advising Christian friends because God sometimes, indeed frequently, chooses to use the objective input of his other servants to impart his guidance.

Priorities. The Christian's top priority is God and his or her relationship with him in Christ. Next comes one's spouse, then children, job, church, and finally one's social life—in that order. This order is biblical, based on the writings in Genesis, the teachings of Jesus, and the admonitions in the letters of Paul and Peter. Any divergence can adversely affect, not only family peace and security, but also an individual's happiness and contentment. The most common disruptions of this order are the husband and father who places job, church, or social life above family in the matter of time commitment, the wife and mother who places her children above her husband or her husband above her commitment to Christ, and the teenager who places social life above responsibilities to parents and siblings.

God has created order, and as Christ was submissive to his Father, so the bride of Christ, made up of Christian families, is to be submissive to his will. Likewise, the husband who is called to be the spiritual head of the family must be submissive to the Lord. The wife who is called to be the bride of her husband should be submissive to him, and the children who are the fruit of the home are called upon to be obedient to their parents. When this order is disobeyed, conflict and disharmony result and lead to unhappiness; love is the characteristic that can maintain order. For the Christian, submission becomes more of a spiritual than a psychological matter. The husband is exhorted to love his wife as Christ loved the church and laid down his life for the church, and she in turn is called upon to submit herself to her husband.

Subjection or submission does not mean slavery, especially in these days of educated women. If a husband, under God, truly loves his wife, she will have nothing to lose by being obedient to him. She will be able to trust that the decisions of a godly husband will be best for herself and the family. In a Christian home, submission should actually be mutual—all yielding to the needs of others.

Time commitment among family members. Husbands and wives *must* be alone together, away from the children, frequently and regularly. I recommend a minimum of at least two to three hours per week. Now this does not mean going to a movie or a concert or to the theater or the opera. The purpose is to talk, listen, share, respond, and communicate. Look into each other's eyes. Call each other by first names, not just "honey" or "darling" or some funny nickname. Revive weekly, even if only for a few fleeting moments, the sense of commitment, the mutual attention, and the total involvement with each other that thrilled you both during your honeymoon and the earliest months of marriage. Discuss the difficulties in the home or differences in approaches to problems. *Never* let disagreements smolder. Bring them out into open discussion, *not* at the moment of conflict, but at a later moment in calm, rational, loving, yielding, and sharing dialogue. Try also to get away alone together for a few days or an occasional weekend every few months. You both need it.

Parents must also discipline and budget time to give children their due. A father must be willing to forego occasional business or social evenings or weekend activities in favor of responsibilities to his children, especially when children are between the ages of seven to twelve, when his influence on them is maximum. A father must always be readily approachable so that his children can share their discoveries and enthusiasms and consult him about their problems. He is the first adult male with whom his sons and daughters will identify, and their early concept of him will distinctly color their later psychosexual developments and their adult relationships with the opposite sex.

Parents must listen to a child's opinions and humble themselves to be patient enough to try to understand his or her point of view. They must respect a child's opinion, explain why they believe theirs is a better course of action, and present it logically at the child's level of understanding so that he or she has a chance to see the alternative viewpoint. Occasionally of course it is necessary for a parent to be authoritative and simply lay down the law. This is especially the case when a child is being manipulative or trying to use illogical arguments to avoid certain responsibilities.

There should be a transparency in the parent-child relationship which permits either to speak freely with the other. It is tragic to hear a young person say, "I can't talk to my parents about it." A major factor in insuring a sense of security in a child is knowledge from experience that no matter what happens in any area of life, he or she can talk to mother or father about it. A child must be able to approach both parents about any subject—problems in school, exams, studies, sports, future college or career, money, friends, social activities, dating, sex. The secure and mature child or adolescent can immediately turn first to his or her home for help when confronted with any unexpected disappointment or need for advice, reassurance, or encouragement.

Mothers of very young children especially should organize their household and other duties so that they can play with their little ones frequently during the day, every day. Those early years pass so quickly and should be filled with parental attention. Baby-sitters, nannys, and governesses are poor substitutes. Attention does not mean only controlling, yelling, or spanking. It involves doing with them what *they* want to do and showing them your enjoyment in sharing their play. However bored you may become with their little games and fantasies, remember that the joy and thrill young children experience during those few precious minutes when they have a parent all to themselves are irreplaceable by any substitute. This ecstasy in the child and the happiness he or she radiates far outweigh the temporary inconvenience or delay of other household obligations.

Parents must teach both by word and by example. The period of latency from ages seven to twelve are the years of character foundation and represent a happy carefree time. The child is old enough to explore and appreciate many of the good and exciting things in his or her world, yet not old enough to have the anxieties and frustrations of the teenage years. A child's mind is developed to the point where he or she is stimulated and aroused by new learning experiences, and he or she therefore needs to be taught to discern between good and bad, safe and dangerous, and socially acceptable and unacceptable. Although the basic *principles* of right and wrong are learned before the age of seven, during the latency years children learn what *is* right and wrong and gain experience in applying practically the principles learned earlier.

During latency children also acquire an early sense of identity and develop their first conscious sense of self-worth. Indeed, one of the fundamental principles of good character foundation is establishing at this time a healthy self-concept which will become the basis of all future interpersonal relationships. Developing ego and the basic cultural skills come preeminently from a child's identification with parents and teachers on whom, therefore, the responsibility for these achievements largely rests.

Between the ages of nine and twelve a child is most receptive to discussions on moral and religious issues. Earlier, he or she will have only limited understanding; later the blooming adolescent mind tends to become confused with intellectual arguments. Given help from parents or Sunday school teachers, a latency-age child will not only learn from, but actually enjoy, reading the Scriptures and praying. He or she can thereby acquire additional resources to influence the development of a solid foundation for the character he or she will have as an adult.

In school, children learn the facts they need to know to become educated persons and are instructed in certain mental and mechanical skills which can enable them to obtain good employment when they grow up. In the home children are instructed in those qualities of life which enable them to develop an attractive personality, a stable temperament, and a reliable and upright character. At home they are taught the right way to do things. Moral and religious principles should be taught primarily in the home, not at school or even in church. All the facts of sex a child needs to know at a particular age should come first from mother and father, and parents are preeminently responsible for insuring that the child knows right from wrong in this and all other areas of life.

With regard to example, remember that actions speak louder than words. If parents spend time with their children, they can teach them a great deal just by doing things together. The quality of parents' lives directly influences the child. Honesty, truthfulness, thoughtfulness, righteous living, keeping promises, maintaining moral principles and ethical standards in all practices, and communicating these virtues by deeds as well as words will give strength and consistency to the child's developing conscience. Parents must be parents, not just pals. A definite authority gap has to be maintained according to God's Word. Children must *never* be allowed to control their parents. Insecurity and indiscipline will inevitably result. The ideal is to control children without stifling or killing their spirits of independence, curiosity, and self-expression.

Parents can also inspire enthusiasm in a wide variety of interests and activities by personal example. Instruction and help with hobbies and encouragement in sports and other indoor and outdoor pursuits can expand horizons and make childhood years exciting and satisfying. This alone will prevent much of the boredom of affluence which leads so often to delinquent behavior in later years. The foundations of a good adult character are laid not only with talk but also with example, not only with teaching but also with living.

The family altar. A Christian home is significantly different from one in which Christ is not honored. The theocratic hierarchy is clearly taught in Scripture: Christ is the Lord of the home, the husband and father the human spiritual leader under Christ, and the wife and children in subjection and obedience to him. In our generation, subjection and obedience do not mean inferior status and servitude. The father's Christian duty is to take on the obligation of spiritual leadership in the home. This in no way negates equality of husband and wife. It is not a matter of who is the boss; it is a matter of sharing various responsibilities.

Paul wrote: "Children, obey your parents in the Lord: for this is right. Honour thy father and mother; . . . And, ye fathers, provoke not your children to wrath: but bring them up in the nurture and admonition of the Lord" (Eph. 6: 1–2, 4).

Many books have been written on how to raise children. All of them can be summed up in one verse from the Bible: "Train up a child in the way he should go: and when he is old, he will not depart from it" (Prov. 22:6). This truth, written about three thousand years ago, probably by King Solomon, has remained the cornerstone of the building of every human character throughout the centuries. The poet Wordsworth wrote that "the child is father of the man," meaning that good or bad qualities developed in childhood directly influence the character produced in adult life.

It is the parents' responsibility to teach their children these basic principles and to lead them to understand clearly the things of God. Children will then be able to make their own decisions about yielding to the authority of Christ as king in their lives. Be careful, however, that God the Father is presented not only as an authority figure but also as God of love, understanding, forgiveness, and providence. If this is done, there will be far less likelihood of children of strict religious parents rebelling in adolescent years. The longer a child lives in a godly home, the greater are his or her chances of embracing a personal faith similar to that of the parents. The longer a child is deprived of basic religious instruction, the less likely he or she is to understand or be influenced by it in adult years.

In the ideal Christian home all members love and serve Christ as their own Lord. Where Christian love and worship of the Lord are the dominant features in the home, the marriage between parents is joyful, peaceful, and mutually satisfying, and the children are nurtured in security and love. Family prayers with Bible reading are the central acts of worship. The whole Scripture should be studied systematically and repeatedly over the years so that the Word of God soaks permanently into the minds and hearts of all family members. Parents should teach their children how to know Christ personally. They should pray *for* their children and *with* their children, mentioning each one by name.

Children should be taught to intercede for one another, for their parents, family, and friends, and to make supplication for their own needs in conformity with God's will for their lives. Repentance, praise, and giving thanks for all things prevent self-centeredness in their prayers.

When conflict arises, the husband, as spiritual leader, should lead his wife and children in prayer about the problem, both privately and as a family. Verbalized prayer is itself good communication. As I speak to God, I am being heard by my wife and children. I must, however, in honesty and truth really be speaking to God in my heart, not using communion with God as a means of continuing an argument with them. Family prayers transacted in humility, with all desiring God's will, can break down many barriers. Selfishness, pride, and greed can be conquered when Christian families sincerely seek God's will. Talking to God together brings a closeness by developing the spiritual dimension of the relationships. Also, prayer often enables members of a family to see when they have been wrong. This can be a very humbling yet deep experience which can lead to greater respect and love for one another.

Forgive and forget: "Be ye angry, and sin not: let not the sun go down upon your wrath" (Eph. 4:26). It requires moral strength to admit being wrong and to ask forgiveness. It requires even more strength to apologize, forgive, and verbalize continuing love when you are perhaps not wrong. Forgiving also means forgetting. If God can forget, so can we. ". . . For I will forgive their iniquity, and I will remember their sin no more" (Jer. 31:34).

Homes in which the love of Christ fills every heart will be homes in which the Holy Spirit controls, inspires, and guides every member and gives power to resist temptation and to live godly lives. This is not an unrealistic ideal. It is the practical reality of a genuine spirituality in many homes today, where submission to Christ has resulted in his loving care for every member, protection from outside danger, and security, fulfillment, peace, and happiness within the walls.

3.

Christian Parenthood

Bruce Narramore

An airline pilot on a nighttime transcontinental flight spoke over the intercom saying, "Ladies and gentlemen, I have some mixed news for you tonight. Some of the news is good and some is bad. First, the bad news—we are low on fuel, our instruments are out, and we have lost our way. Now for the good news—I am happy to report we are making excellent time!"

I believe many modern parents share this pilot's mixed emotions. They have an ideal goal or destination for their children, but they are not sure how to get there. At times they feel completely lost. In spite of poor directions, however, they know they are making excellent time. In a few short years some destination will be reached. Their children will be grown, and the opportunity to make an impact on their lives will be forever lost. Looking back, many of these parents will see they needed better guidance.

Those in places of Christian leadership are in excellent positions to offer this direction. To do this, however, we must have a deep sensitivity to the problems parents face and a clear understanding of ways to help them cope with the demanding tasks of parenthood.

As I travel around, I find certain questions consistently on the

---

Dr. Bruce Narramore is academic dean of the Rosemead Graduate School of Psychology. He is the author of several books including, *Help I'm a Parent*, and *An Ounce of Prevention*.

minds of Christian parents. Parents of rebellious adolescents most often ask, "Where did we go wrong?" or "Why do teenagers from 'fine Christian families' rebel?" From slightly less-conflicted families I hear questions like, "How do you get a teenager to communicate?" Parents of younger children ask about practical daily hassles: "How do you stop a temper tantrum?" "How do you get children out of bed and off to school each morning?" "How do you get a finicky child to eat a balanced diet?" "How do you stop children from fighting?" and "How do you get children to take out the trash or feed the dog?" I also hear a whole range of questions about behaviors that border on the pathological: "Why is my child so withdrawn and unable to communicate?" "Why does one of my children have such an uncontrollable temper?" and "Why is our teenager flunking when we know he has at least average intellectual ability?"

Inherent in these questions are several primary concerns. Christian parents are really asking: How can we insure our children's moral and spiritual growth? How can we handle daily family conflicts and frustrations? How can we help our children grow up to be emotionally healthy? These are important questions. The church should be able to help its members insure the future emotional and spiritual stability of their youth, and it should be able to help parents cope with the frustrating daily hassles that occasionally trouble us all. But I believe there is one more basic question: Does the Bible give us a realistic set of guidelines for raising children, and if so, what is it?

During the past twenty years great changes have occurred in the attitude of the church toward the parents in its assembly. Prior to that time there were practically no good books on Christian parenting. Our Sunday school curricula, while occasionally dealing with the subject, typically overlooked this crucial area of life. Parenting was thought to be a tangential concern. It was elective material (not really to be placed in the center of study), but with the growing influence of psychology and a national concern for the family, all of this is changing. Books on the family are consistently among the national religious bestsellers. Psychologists, educators, pastors, and members of dozens of other professions have started ministering to the Christian parent.

Frankly, I view this movement with mixed emotions. It is clearly responding to the deep and vital needs within the church today, and much of the material is helpful. Unfortunately, as is so often the case, the emphasis on the family is growing to almost faddish proportions. It seems that everyone who has had a child (and some who haven't) now fancies himself or herself an expert in the field. In preparing this paper I read through several relatively recent Christian books and papers on rearing children. The lack of consensus was amazing. One pamphlet (published in four languages) purporting to give a biblical view of discipline has this to say about physical spanking:

> My obedience to God to train my child requires that every time I ask him to do something, whatever it is, I must see that he obeys. When I have said it once in a normal tone, if he does not obey immediately, I must take up the switch and correct him enough to hurt so he will not want it repeated.[1]

In contrast another Christian writes: "There are too many people running around with a biblical two by four who really don't know very much of what the Scriptures teach regarding discipline."[2] Regarding motivation, one author said that fear was the one great emotion to which children would respond.[3] Another felt that love should be the primary motive.[4]

Needless to say this kind of contradiction leaves the man on the street in a very confused position. What is *really* right? Who holds the correct answers? Is Christianson right? Is Dobson right? Is Gothard right? Is Hendricks right? Is Lovett right? Is Narramore right? The truth is that no one is entirely right. Each of us approaches the task of childrearing from personal biases and preconceived notions. As much as I hate to admit it, this is certainly true of me. While I try to be sensitive to my own needs and biases, I cannot claim infallibility for my perspectives on the parent-child relationship. This focuses on one major problem in rising to the needs of Christian parents. We must carefully avoid taking either our own subjective experience or the subjective experience of secular psychologists and baptizing them with selected verses in order to claim the authority of God.

This leads to my first specific suggestion for changing the

quality of living in the Christian home. *We desperately need a theology of childrearing.* No longer can we be satisfied with a three-point theology that says, "Husbands love your wives; wives submit to your husbands; and children obey your parents." While important, these commands contain only a very small part of the biblical view of family interactions. If we are to constrain our tendency toward subjectively derived childrearing approaches, we must arrive at a thoroughly comprehensive and biblical view of parenting. There are over five thousand references in the Bible using the words *father* and *son.* On top of this, one of the Bible's central themes is God's fatherly relationship with Israel. In the New Testament a number of passages speak of the parallels between earthly fathers and the heavenly Father. Surely all these passages hold a rich treasure for the parent of today, but I am not aware of one truly comprehensive biblical treatise on parenting that takes most of these Scriptures into account. The following discussion illustrates the type of scriptural insight I believe is available.

Christian parents are to look at God's relationship to them as a model for their relationships with their children. Passages like Hebrews 12:3–11 and Matthew 7:9–11 point out this parallel. If we carefully study how God as heavenly Father relates to us as earthly children, we should find some very clear principles for parent-child relationships.

For example, in God's dealings with man there is a clear distinction between punishment, as a means of administering retribution for misdeeds, and discipline, which is designed to promote the growth of the disciplined one. God never punishes his own children. All his righteous demands were met by Christ's atoning death on the cross. Once we accept Christ as personal Savior, we receive no more punishment. Instead, we are disciplined, chastened, or corrected. This is a crucial distinction and is often overlooked. Discipline is not a means of justice. Justice has already been satisfied. Discipline is God's way of *maturing* his children. It is instruction or training designed to correct misbehavior and develop the disciplined one. It doesn't involve justice, punishment, or getting even.

Based on this theological distinction between God's discipline and his punishment, I would suggest that the Christian parent should *never* punish his or her child. We should discipline, but we should never punish. The chart below summarizes some of the major distinctions.[5] I believe understanding these differences is as important for the effective traning of children as it is for our own walk with the heavenly Father.

Due to the complexity of the task, a useful theology of parent-child relations must be biblically comprehensive. It must include attention to biblical anthropology, for example, since the way we view man influences our entire approach to discipline and child training. If children are basically good, a permissive or democratic approach to childrearing may be justified. If, on the other hand, we view man as basically evil, we will not find these approaches consistent with our theology of man. And if we accept a third alternative (the one I believe is biblical) that man is best viewed as created in the image of God and subsequently fallen, we will have a different view than if we emphasize either man's "goodness" or "badness" at the expense of a biblically balanced perspective.

	PUNISHMENT	DISCIPLINE
PURPOSE	To inflict penalty for an offense. (2 Thessalonians 1:7-9)	To train for correction and maturity (Proverbs 3:11, 12)
FOCUS	Past misdeeds (Matthew 25:46)	Future correct deeds (Hebrews 12:5 10)
ATTITUDE OF THE PARENT	Anger (Isaiah 13:9 11)	Loving concern (Revelation 3:19)
RESULTING EMOTION IN THE CHILD	Fear, guilt and hostility	Security and respect (Hebrews 9:28)

This third view of man leads to a view of childrearing that errs neither on the side of permissiveness (since it recognizes man's sinful nature) nor on the side of authoritarianism (since it recognizes that all children, in spite of their sinfulness, still bear the stamp and the image of the Creator). In place of the extremes of permissiveness and authoritarianism we can develop the biblical model that children are people of worth and value but that they also need lovingly exercised authority to counter their sinful bent and see them through the growing years of childhood.

A theology of childrearing must also give attention to theology proper, the nature and attributes of God. Only as we fully grasp the implications of God's character for our own lives can we attempt to model his character in our relations with our children.

Theologians speak, for example, of God's immutability. He never changes. Parents, of course, must change—hopefully for the better—but what a challenge to consistent parenting a recognition of God's immutability can be! One reason we can feel secure in God's love is that he is consistent—he never changes. Similarly a study of God's holiness, righteousness, love, mercy, grace, and truth should make us think twice about our reactions to our children. What does it mean to act in truth toward our children? Do we, in our relationships with them, communicate truth and grace? Or do we communicate subtle forms of dishonesty and an unforgiving spirit?

Ecclesiology is also fertile ground for the aspiring parent. Since a major mission of the church is the edification and maturation of its members (Eph. 4:1–13), the principles of growth, relationships, and change that are laid out for the church in Scripture can certainly give us insights into the process of growth that our children must pass through. And what about soteriology? What effect does the fact that our children have undergone a salvation experience have on our view of them and on our discipline?

I personally believe that nearly every branch of theology holds important teaching for effective parenting. I would suggest that until we have studied many of these teachings we should not claim to have a truly biblical view of childrearing. We may be on the right track, and we may have a great deal of biblical truth, but we will not have gone as far as we can in applying the riches of God's Word to the needs of contemporary parents.

A second need for an effective ministry to parents is trained church leaders who understand basic principles of discipline and childrearing, who are sensitive to the feelings and needs of both parents and children, and who are qualified to conduct training sessions for parents. I realize this is easier said than done, but I believe it is vitally important. We need men and women within our churches who have had sufficient life experience to be sensitive to the feelings of parents and their children and who are also sufficiently schooled in the biblical view of parenting that they are not driven from pillar to post by their own subjective reasoning or that of persons confronting them with problems. These people must have the maturity to hold out high goals without placing themselves "above" other learners. They must also be able to encourage honest and open sharing rather than creating a critical environment that reinforces feelings of guilt and failure.

Needless to say, I do not see today's seminary curriculum training this sort of Christian leader. Most divinity students do not have as much as one course on the Christian family, let alone an entire course on parent-child relationships. While I am not suggesting that every minister should be competent to lead a seminar on Christian parenting, somebody has to do it, and these people will need training.

Can our seminaries be expected to assume this responsibility? Frankly, I am not sure. I am afraid too much seminary education is divorced from real life issues. Hebrew, Greek, theology, church history, homiletics, and English Bible are obviously important to the training of a minister, but Jesus was "touched with the *feelings* of our infirmities." What in our seminary curriculum helps prospective pastors become sensitive to the *feelings* of a rebellious adolescent, a fearful eight-year-old, a stubborn two-year-old, an anxious mother, or a disinterested father? Very little, I suspect. And perhaps this shouldn't be the seminaries' role, but if the seminary doesn't do it, who will? I believe we should set up institutes for training pastors and other leaders for parent ministries. Either within the seminary or in some other setting we need thorough training experiences that ground people in the biblical view of parenting *plus* help them become sensitive to the feelings and infirmities of parent and child alike. This, of course, presupposes the personnel to train future leaders.[6]

A third need is new material for Christian parents. Although much of value has been produced in recent years, I think that we still do not have any clearly definitive works that lay out a complete biblical foundation for parenting and then practically apply that foundation to the myriad of problems faced by the average parent.

We need action-centered material. We need programs, workbooks, and planned activities that will help parents apply basic biblical and psychological insights to daily family problems. It is not enough to simply state the principles. The life-long habit patterns of most parents rarely change with a few intellectual insights or prophetic exhortation. Instead, they change only when we have consistent support and guidance from other people.

For example, I find it quite easy to go into a church or large group meeting and speak for an hour or two on parent-child relationships. I can entertain the audience. I can give new biblical and psychological insights. And I think people generally go away feeling they have received their money's worth! But I sometimes walk away with a certain empty feeling. I realize that when the sun comes up the next morning most people who heard my lecture won't really be so very different in relating to their children. Oh, they may have some new insights, and they may try a couple of new "techniques," but few really deep, basic changes will have taken place. It is one thing, for example, to tell a parent he or she should not correct children in anger or attack their self-esteem. It is quite another for that parent to gain sufficient insight into his or her own hostilities to avoid punishing instead of disciplining or to avoid demeaning a child's sense of self-esteem. This is certainly true in my experience with my own children.

The Scriptures make it clear that growth is a process and that we need other people to provoke it (Eph. 4:14–16). Most of us can change if we have someone who can stick with us over a period of time to allow us to express our feelings and frustrations, to help us gain a greater measure of objectivity, and gradually to improve our parenting behavior, but most parents don't have this opportunity. They attend a lecture or read a book, and then they are on their own. This should not be.

I am often asked to recommend books and materials that will be of help to parents. Frankly, I hesitate to recommend any specific material because I have yet to find anything I agree with completely! I have also been unable to read all of the materials that are available. Given these limitations, I think what might be most helpful is a set of guidelines to evaluate both the accuracy and the practicality of the many available materials.

First, the material should clearly reflect the viewpoint that the Bible is our ultimate authority. By this I do not mean that the material has to have hundreds of biblical references. The number of biblical references is not nearly as important as the basic tone of the material. Satan can quote Scripture! Does the author communicate a deep commitment to the inspiration and authority of the Scriptures? And do his writings appear to flow from this commitment and from a desire to communicate God's truth about the family? Or does he engage more in an occasional prooftexting of essentially secular theories?

Second, what is the author's view of family government? Is it permissive? Is it authoritarian? Or is it biblical? As I understand the Bible, it lays out a family structure based upon mutual sensitivity and sharing within the framework of the loving authority of the parents. Specifically, I do not see the Bible supporting either the "because I said so" approach of authoritarianism or the "if it feels good do it" approach of permissiveness. As the model parent, God does not force us to do a lot of things we do not want. He is amazingly patient and understanding of our feelings. At the same time he does not leave us to our own desires and devices with no firm guidance or direction. Materials that lean to either of these extremes should be considered suspect.

Third, the author's view of motivation should be biblical. By that I mean that the major means of parental motivation should be love and an understanding of the consequences of negative behaviors. Writings that promote the use of parental power to instill fear in a child are not acceptable. Consider this quotation as an example:

> If I were to ask, "Which emotion should fathers and mothers use to counter Satan's appeals?" You'd come back with the sweet reply—"LOVE." That sounds very nice and proper, doesn't it? Well, I'm sorry—that's NOT the emotion. We need something more powerful than parental love. There's only one emotion that is greater—FEAR. I know that startles you. But mama-love and papa-love do not have the same effect on them it used to.
>
> Parents, seeking to compete with Satan, must answer with the countering emotion of fear. Fear is the one great emotion to which everyone responds. Fear alone can check the awesome forces unleashed in teens.[7]

Biblical discipline is based on the loving response of an understanding parent, not the angry one of a frustrated adult. As John put it, "There is no fear in love, but perfect love casts out fear. For fear has to do with punishment, and he who fears is not perfected in love" (1 John 4:18, RSV). Our appeals to changed behavior should be based on love and an understanding of the harmful consequences that misbehavior causes rather than on fear. A. H. Strong includes an excellent discussion of the theological distinctions between discipline and punishment in his *Systematic Theology*.[8]

Fourth, helpful writings on parent-child relationships should reflect the author's understanding of the child's inner world. To borrow a term from secular psychology, they should reflect the author's ability to assume the child's "internal frame of reference." Does the author understand what it must be like to be a hungry infant lying in a crib? Does he understand what it must be like to be a fearful two-year-old in a world of seeming giants? Or, does the author see things only from adult perspectives? For example, it is so easy to see the two-year-old simply as a "stubborn, rebellious child." It is much more difficult to understand why he is so stubborn—two years ago he didn't even exist; one year ago he was just beginning to walk and talk; now he feels hopelessly small and inadequate and his stubbornness reflects, not only his rebellious nature, but also a wholesome desire to become a person in his own right. Similarly, does the author know teen-agers are *supposed* to be "moody" and to bounce from one at-titude or activity to another?

Fifth, the author of good material for parents should show a mature sensitivity to his or her own attitudes and feelings. If someone is really an expert, he or she won't claim to have *all* the answers and will not be rigid in attitudes and actions.

Sixth, materials for parents should be immensely practical. While homiletical excellence may be fine for the pulpit, eloquent persuasion does little to change the life-style of the twentieth-century parent. We need materials that tell us how to handle temper tantrums, sibling fights, the finicky eater, the rebellious adolescent, and the spiritual dropout. Materials that fail to touch such practical issues as these are best left on the shelves.

I am sure I could go on and list several other guidelines, and, frankly, I could probably rule out all material, including my own! This is not what I intend. Instead, I am suggesting that we try to select the best possible material, but we should be prepared to evaluate it critically and not hesitate to correct its inad-equacies through additional reading, exercises, or lecture input.

For example, I frequently refer parents to Rudolf Dreikurs's *Logical Consequences: A New Approach to Discipline*[9] and Haim Ginott's *Between Parent and Child.*[10] These secular books both have a very inadequate view of the nature of man and of the biblical pattern for family government, but Ginott's is the best book I know on communication with children, and Dreikurs's presentation of natural and logical consequences is superb. I tell parents, "Ginott is beautiful on communication but wretched on discipline, and Dreikurs is great on natural and logical conse-quences, but his concepts of democracy and of the nature of man are grossly unbiblical!" If we are willing to be creative and criti-cal, we can all find material to adapt to our particular needs and purposes.

A fourth primary need for changing the quality of living in the Christian home has to do with the program of the local church. *We need to structure classes and seminars into the on-*

going educational outreach of our churches. I personally believe that every church should have at least one full quarter class for parents each year. This could be during the Sunday school hour, on Sunday evening, or during the week, but it should be a vital part of the church's Christian education program. Ideally, it should not be an elective that is offered *after* church members have taken other basic courses. It should be at the very heart and core of our entire Christian education program. What an opportunity to make our theology relevant! What better way to learn something of the character of God than to study the implications of God's dealings with us as his children for our dealing with our own children? What greater opportunity to understand and appropriate God's forgiveness than to think of forgiving our own children? And what better way to see God's loving hand of discipline than to begin to see the difference between the times we lovingly correct our children for their good and the times we punish them out of our own frustration?

These classes or seminars need to be structured to maximize participation. It is not enough to hear the principles. We need individual or small-group attention and support to apply the principles to *our* children in *our* situation. Small study groups serve as ideal vehicles for taking a theology of childrearing, communicating it through a trained leader and appropriate materials, and weaving it into the fabric of daily living. These groups take important principles from the realm of the abstract and put them into practice.

As a psychologist I see one other basic need. This is for *a series of comprehensive research studies into the workings of the Christian home.* By singling out certain obviously effective Christian parents and studying their relations with their children, perhaps we could gain insight into some essential ingredients of effective parenting. Do emotionally mature and spiritually committed children come from homes where the father spends a great deal of time with the children? Do they come from homes that have daily family devotions? Do they come from families that rely heavily on physical spanking? Do they come from families with good husband-wife communication? Or is the overall emotional tone of the family the most important factor?

And what is going on in the many apparently "fine Christian homes" that have produced rebellious, spiritually disinterested children? Was an unseen authoritarianism at work? Were the parents so busy in church activities the children felt neglected? Or did the children feel an excessive need to "be good" because they were held out as an exemplary Christian family? Answers to these and similar questions could be very helpful in shedding new light on effective parenting.

Some recently initiated research studies at the Rosemead Graduate School of Psychology illustrate another type of research that can be helpful. Fleck and Day[11] studied the relationship between the perceptions a group of college students had of God and of their parents. They found that college students who were converted prior to ten years of age had very similar God and parent concepts while students converted at age seventeen or older showed much less similarity.

In a related study Edwards[12] found a positive relationship between the image of God a group of college students had and the quality of their spiritual experience. Taken together these two studies demonstrate two important principles: (1) A person's image of God is apparently a function of the way he perceives his earthly parents, and (2) This image of God is related to the quality of the person's spiritual experience. The implications are wide-ranging. If a child has unforgiving parents, he is likely to see God as unforgiving. If he has perfectionistic parents, he will probably have difficulty believing God is ever pleased with his performance. And if he has a nagging parent, he will tend to view God as being constantly "on his back." I believe confusion of God and parent is one of the major causes of spiritual rebellion among adolescents. They blame God for their parents' failings, identify God with their parents, and rebel against both. This vicious cycle can be changed only as parents give children a healthier image of what God is like through their daily relations with their children.

In another study, Foster and Edwards[13] found that parents

from Christian homes were a more important source of influence in the development of their children's self-esteem than non-Christian parents. Although children from Christian homes showed no higher levels of self-esteem than those from non-Christian homes, their parents did make a greater impact (for better or worse) on their children's self-esteem! This study also raises some important questions. Why, for example, didn't children from Christian homes evidence a higher level of self-esteem than those from non-Christian homes? And why is it that Christian parents apparently have a greater impact on their children's self-esteem than non-Christian parents? I won't venture any answers at this point but would like to suggest we need to find some answers.

These studies only scratch the surface, but they indicate the type of information that is available. Many more practical problems can be researched. We could, for example, study the effects of the separation of missionary children from their parents. We could study the effects of parents' personality styles on the adjustment of children, and we could study the effect of church attendance and peer influence on Christian children.

A final area of research could be the effectiveness of various training programs for parents. What lasting effects come, for example, from attendance at the many types of conferences and seminars now being offered? Do family conferences really change the family? And do seminars for parents really change the parents? An evaluation of several types of training programs could tell us what type of training really works. We may currently be wasting a lot of time in unproductive efforts. If so, we should eliminate them. On the other hand, if some programs are working, let's find out why and how and begin to utilize them even more productively.

These are just a few areas that call for our attention. A topic as complex as Christian parenthood really deserves much lengthier study. I do believe, however, that if we develop a theology of childrearing, a group of trained leaders, practical new materials, structured classes and seminars, and a series of comprehensive research studies we will be well on our way to a vastly improved ministry to parents.

NOTES

1. Al and Pat Fabrijio, *Children—Fun or Frenzy?* (Palo Alto, Cal.: a pamphlet, 1969), p. 10.

2. Howard G. Hendricks, *Heaven Help the Home* (Wheaton, Ill.: Victor Books, 1974), p. 67.

3. C. S. Lovett, *What's a Parent to Do?* (New York: Personal Christianity, 1971), p. 61.

4. Hazen G. Werner, "Wise Parental Love," *The Marriage Affair*, ed. J. Allan Peterson (Wheaton, Ill.: Tyndale, 1971), pp. 161–62.

5. This material is adapted from my book *Help! I'm a Parent* (Grand Rapids, Michigan: Zondervan, 1972).

6. Other faculty members from the Rosemead Graduate School of Psychology and I have developed an intensive one-week seminar to train pastors, educators, and other interested adults to conduct seminars and classes for parents. This seminar includes approximately 40 hours of instruction as well as collateral reading and curriculum materials that can be used either in the church or in parent study-groups. Information can be obtained by writing Parent Education Seminars, Rosemead Graduate School of Psychology, Rosemead, Cal. 91770.

7. Lovett, *What's a Parent to Do?* p. 61.

8. A. H. Strong, *Systematic Theology* (Old Tappan, N.J.: Fleming H. Revell, 1916), pp. 652–55.

9. Rudolf Dreikurs, *Logical Consequences: A New Approach to Discipline* (New York: Hawthorn 1968).

10. Haim Ginott, *Between Parent and Child* (New York: Avon, 1965).

11. J. R. Fleck, L. G. Day, J. W. Reilly, "Concepts of God and Parents, and Perceived Parental Religious Orientation as a Function of Age of Christian Conversion Experience," 1974.

12. K. J. Edwards, "Sex-Role Stereotyping of Jesus: A Dimension of Identification and Its Relation to Subjective Religious Experience," 1975.

13. T. Foster and K. J. Edwards, "Parental Influences on Self-Esteem of Preadolescent Boys in Evangelical and Nonevangelical Families," 1975.

4.

Integrating Teenagers into the Family

Jay Kesler

The topic of integrating teenagers into the family raises some interesting questions. For example, which teenagers? If we assume a teenager who has been raised in an atmosphere of Christian grace, discipline, and love, then we might also assume that we are dealing with a young person who has a positive attitude about authority structures. If, on the other hand, we assume a teenager who is the product of an unhappy home or a nonreligious, non-Christian family, we would make some altogether different assumptions about his or her attitude toward self and others.

Since it is important to place observations and judgments in the proper context, I acknowledge that my specific frame of reference will be teenagers and their families as I generally perceive them in the evangelical culture. One should not suppose, however, that all evangelical teenagers come from a typical, so-called "Christian" home. Within this classification are a broad range of options and life-styles ranging from arbitrary, inflexible, militaristic dictatorships to intimidated, relativistic, sideless anarchies.

The term *integration*, as it is most popularly used today, di-

---

Jay Kesler is president of Youth for Christ International. He is the author of two books, *Let's Succeed with Our Teenagers*, and *I Never Promised You a Disneyland*.

rectly applies to the matter of integrating teens into family life. A half-dozen preschool-age children of various racial backgrounds placed on a playground will "integrate" in an amazing way in a few minutes. It won't take long for those who don't know how to swing to learn from the swingers or for the sliders to teach the not-yet-sliders. In the same way, the family is God's idea, and apart from learned negative attitudes on the part of adults and teens, it is natural for children and teens to be integrated into family life.

Respect of Persons above Institutions

We have just come through a period in America when many young people opted out of their own families to commit themselves to alternatives such as communes, street living, radical political movements, the occult, Eastern religions, drugs. Many felt that their homes either lacked some basic commitment to persons and community or were compromised by "the system" until even good people like their parents were unable to act as individuals. Some felt that their very lives could be a counterculture statement. I doubt that any American family has escaped the effect of this statement.

Our response to counterculture and change is very much tied to whether or not teens are integrated into family life. Because they have all been more or less enculturated by these questions, we must get to the root causes and attempt to meet them there. These questions really have to do with the individual versus the system. In the larger sense, teens question whether parents view persons as ends in themselves. Teens today view people as creatures of God and important, not as means to an end of serving institutions, whether political, industrial, church, or military (some even view the family as institutional). Jacques Ellul has dealt with this problem prophetically and in depth in *The Presence of the Kingdom.*[1]

To the degree that youth sense that family dignifies personhood, and often selfishly their own personhood, they desire to be part of it. Young people will naturally gravitate toward a certain family climate. In the creation of this climate and in the consistent specific actions that validate this climate, healthy relationships will develop.

AN OPEN ATTITUDE

Young people are constantly picking up new ideas and information. Much of it is the result of exposure to the world and its influences, good and bad, through media, the classroom, personal experiences, and opinions of friends. When they bring these ideas home and find them rejected "out of hand" with no compelling logic or attempt at understanding, they often decide to save the hassle and leave parents and family out of their personal life. A Chicago-based agency dealing with runaways (they would seem least integrated into family life) lists the most often given reason by youth for running away as "they quit listening to me." Young people today are taught to ask *why*. They expect there to be a reason. If none is given, they suspect parents of being arbitrary, ignorant, afraid, or less sophisticated. "That's the way it is, why try to share with them?"

It takes some faith to believe that the Christian message with its specific and implied moral code has a rationale. It often takes some effort to examine both Scripture and experience to find it, but when young people learn that parents are committed to dispassionate, unafraid, confident discussion in a spirit of openness and humility, with growing confidence they will share their experiences and ideas. My daughter, a voracious reader, recently brought home a book titled *The Bastard*. The cover proclaimed to me that it was a good novel, and, besides, it was part of some bicentennial effort. Somehow though I wasn't very comforted by these marketing and patriotic assurances. The title seemed a little stiff for a fifteen-year-old even though it is a good King James word. My immediate response was to look for reviews on the back cover. Finding none, I suggested that 750 pages is a lot of effort if the book is no good. She has, however, this year read: *A Day in the Life of Ivan Denisovich, Exodus, Battle Cry, Mila 18, Armageddon, Cry, the Beloved Country, A Tale of Two Cities*, and some others I'm not aware of, as well as school assignments. Realizing there might be some specific material to which

I would object and also realizing that she is exposed to life at the local high school and through TV, magazines, and selected movies (and the previews they throw in), I said, "Let's read this book together and talk about it."

This approach has initiated many discussions. Some are quite beyond me, but I would rather talk with her in light of our Christian commitment than drive her to secret places. To integrate reading and intellectual life into our family takes some effort. I think it's worth it. As Winston Churchill said of the United Nations, "Better jaw, jaw, jaw than war, war, war."

TRUST

A number of studies have been done on the general subject of "student performance based on teacher expectation." They are set up to determine whether a teacher's attitude toward his or her students affects their grades, conduct, and social adjustment. "The results indicate strongly that children from whom teachers expected great intellectual gain showed such gains."[2] The results are astonishingly convincing that students tend to perform as they are expected. This is separate from the fact that the teachers try to treat all students the same. Facial expressions, a raised eyebrow, a sigh, tone of voice, touch, all seem to convey some expectation. A child raised in an atmosphere of suspicion and distrust will often feel, "What's the use?" As several have told me, "If that's the way they think, I am sure that's the way I'm going to be."

Teenagers need to be given chances to succeed or fail. A young person who is pampered, overprotected, or untrusted, even for good motives like Christian parental love, will disengage from the family stream to try his or her wings. Opportunities within the home structure with a few carefully built-in safety devices will help to meet both the child's need for independence and the family's responsibility for guidance and protection. If the first time a boy is away from home is college or the army, or if the first time a girl is alone with her friends is at a sorority party, it's too late.

The process of trust must start very early in life. Simple chores with accompanying words of praise or displeasure will build "trustworthiness." Without these opportunities, the whole cause-and-effect consequence is lost, and the benefit of God's natural law is unavailable to our children. Words like *responsibility* lose all meaning unless opportunities to be responsible are given. Teens want to be part of a climate where they are seen as capable and trustworthy. If they can't find it at home, they will find it elsewhere. My observation is that the greater tendency in Christian families is to be immobilized by fear rather than to have faith in God and their children. This produces a well-intentioned but nonetheless negative atmosphere. The antidote is for parents to trust their good judgment, the visibility of Christian teaching, the power of God, and their own children's good sense and character. Taking some risks will bring about great desire on the part of children to trust their parents and to perform to their expectation. There is more to be gained than lost by trust.

ACCEPTANCE OF INDIVIDUALITY

Estranged youth often say, "I'm just not what they expected," or "I can't be what he wants me to be." Even a casual look at today's teens will give a hint that many time-worn, accepted views of what a young man or woman should do or look like have changed. I had three illustrations of this on my way to work one morning. First I saw a young man about eighteen emerge from an excavation beside the road with a construction helmet and long blond curls hanging down below his shoulders. Then I saw a girl, perhaps twenty, with an orange vest holding a surveyor's rod as one member of a road survey team. Within a mile I saw a teenage girl in jeans with a backpack, hitchhiking.

These occurrences are commonplace today and hardly deserve notice. That's the point. The construction crew has integrated long hair into their group. Women are doing many jobs heretofore reserved for men. Girls hitchhiking get no more attention than girls smoking a generation ago. Some of these changes are positive, some are negative, all must be accommodated or dealt with.

Families must come to terms with teenage differences. All boys do not need to play some sport. All children do not need to go to college to be successful. Shoes are intrinsically of no greater value than sandals. All girls do not have to be married to be happy. Many of these are not differences between bad or good, desirable or undesirable, successful or unsuccessful, or even Christian or non-Christian. They are simply differences of choice or often style. If a family rejects these differences, refuses to show interest, puts acceptance or rejection as conditions, or morally weighs these differences, the teenager will often seek an environment that appears to him to examine things in greater depth. This is not to say we do not have preferences, that conventional dress, conduct, education, and vocations do not have merit; it is simply to say we must make room for these to be challenged.

When asked why they hang around certain people or places, almost invariably teens will say, "They respect me, they accept me for myself, I feel comfortable here." A family is a place where members should feel comfortable. Teens can sense rejection of themselves, their friends, their music, dress, ideas. Some people are unable to separate the person from his habits, ideas, clothing, and so on and thus unknowingly drive youth away or to silence or estrangement within the home. When these differences are not of substantive moral value, the degree to which we accept them often determines how much involvement the young person will have in the home and also how tolerant he or she will be of our differences.

DISCIPLINE

A great many parents seem to feel that discipline will drive a wedge between them and their children. Others seem to feel that discipline will stifle creativity or spontaneity. Some overdiscipline and create fearful perfectionists afraid to act for fear of failure. In such cases, the teenager often has an improper concept of authority structures. The underdisciplined teenager usually feels insecure and has contempt for adults and authority. The overdisciplined young person often wants to have a fling or, in words from another generation, "sow wild oats."

I would agree with those who feel that from birth to ten or eleven years rather well-formed boundaries must be established with appropriate rewards and punishments, including sensitively applied physical discipline. From about eleven or twelve to fourteen or fifteen, children are greatly influenced by example and leader-oriented activities. The Boy Scouts of America probably understand more about this age group than any other and have appropriately built around adult models. By the time youth reach fifteen or sixteen, physical discipline becomes impractical. The basic behavior patterns are already established, and attitudes are set which are almost unchangeable. I would not include the great attitudinal changes which sometimes accompany conversion to Christ; however, patterns long established are stubborn to change.

> Adolescence is the period when the underlying core of conscience laid down in the early years is most needed. This is a time of necessary rebellion—when superimposed values seem fake and artificial. The individual self becomes all-important. . . . It [the search] involves experimenting with new ideas, new ways of behavior, and different ways of dressing, and the trying out of new goals and ambitions; but always as the limiter of action there remains the basic core of conscience provided by childhood training from the parents, which prevents completely self-defeating or self-destructive behavior. This core of conscience does need some reinforcing, however, during adolescence. Parents and schools still must show by their rules and restrictions that they will not tolerate infractions of certain basic principles such as those relating to sex, alcohol and crime. They cannot totally abdicate their role as a potential source of pain and punishment, but in general this role must be reserved for major issues.[3]

Discipline for teenagers must take a more adult approach but must be present for a teen really to feel loved and to feel secure. An arbitrary statement about what time to be home, for instance, may accomplish the opposite goal from integrating a young person into family life. A discussion of each activity with reasonable times established related to the event, distance, companions, and day of the week will serve as a better guideline and will be appreciated. Young people often need help to say no to their friends. Sometimes leaning on a decision made by parents can be a great relief to an uncomfortable teenager. Understanding, love, and fairness accompanied by affirmation build strong ties. Young people need acceptance of themselves, if not their conduct. They need forgiveness that understands that the embarrassment of failure is usually strong enough without an "I told you so" thrown in for good measure. Young people are getting ready for adulthood. How are adults disciplined? Primarily by cause and effect. This is a scriptural idea—"whatsoever a man soweth, that shall he also reap." This reality does not cause us to love God less but more. So it is with youth. Love prompts far more than the law demands. Loving discipline will result in youth's willing integration into family life.

The Family, the Teenager, and the Local Church

In today's culture, many youth do not experience on a daily basis the values and benefits of the expanded family. Uncles and aunts, grandmas and grandpas, and cousins live in other parts of the country. They are often strangers. For this reason the local church, made up of brothers and sisters in Christ, can provide with our permission and involvement the aunts and uncles, the substitute grandparents, and the supportive influences often present in a former generation. This "expanded family" can perform vital functions of support for the "nuclear family" alone in a crowded metropolitan sprawl. Caring adults, peers, models, conflict, love, and disappointment are all available in the local church and are a great help in integrating teens into family life. Often a substitute uncle or aunt can interpret our relationship with our teens. These substitute parents can often "stand in the gap." For instance, what eighteen-year-old boy desperately in love can believe that his parents' reluctance is born of real love and concern? More often he feels, "They just don't understand." A caring brother nearer the boy's age in the local congregation may be able to present the same case in a less subjective manner.

Healthy climatic characteristics cause teenagers to be interested in the family and develop willing and loving ties. The following specific suggestions are ideas to build upon in creating a home in which young people feel affirmed, loved, and trusted.

1. Involve teens in financial affairs of the family. Perhaps let them handle the family checkbook for six months.
2. Bring up for discussion every decision which involves the

family, and talk about how it hits the whole group, for example, change of home and disruption of school and friends.

3. Institute a family night and let various members decide what would be a good time.
4. Take individual children out alone with mom or dad for special attention on a regular basis.
5. Never miss an opportunity to affirm or commend a child for a job well done.
6. Compliment good manners, thoughtful actions, and "good" dress whenever they occur.
7. Use dinners and rides in the car for opportunities to express opinions. Start questions with "What do you think about . . . ?" or "How do you feel about . . . ?" more often than "Where were you . . . ?" or "How much did you . . . ?" or "When did you . . . ?"
8. Sanctify holidays and make them special family times when all those present and those absent are loved, missed, and contacted. A phone call at Easter to a teen at Daytona will be appreciated as much as a call on Mother's Day from a teen at college.
9. Give certain assignments with no supervision and expect that they will be carried out on time and well done.
10. Pray much in private for your teenagers, ask forgiveness in public, and remember what it was actually like when you wanted to run away from home. Remember the family is God's idea, and it is not likely he would ask us to do the impossible.

NOTES

1. Jacques Ellul, *The Presence of the Kingdom* (New York: Seabury Press, 1967).

2. Robert Rosenthal and Lenore F. Jacobson, "Teacher Expectations for the Disadvantaged," *Scientific American* (April 1968), p. 48.

3. Graham B. Blaine, Jr., *Youth and the Hazards of Affluence* (New York: Harper & Row, 1966), p. 63.

5.

Family Financial Planning

Waldo J. Werning

A nine-year-old girl who opened a bank account for the first time was asked to fill out an application blank. Required to list her previous bank, she wrote, "Piggy."

Far too many people stay in the piggy-bank stage of financial planning and get into many difficulties as they continually flounder. Who has been advising such church members? Mostly, no one, or secular advisors have counseled people in trouble. However, the basics of Christianity must operate in financial planning as well as all other areas of family life.

Alfred Haake, late economic consultant for General Motors, once stated, "The answers to the problems of economics are found in Christianity." Aristotle wrote on economics; so did Plato, but long before, God had told man, "Work and produce."

Economics is necessary for human survival. The materialism of the Christian message can be observed in the biblical doctrine of creation; God brought matter into existence for a purpose. Christianity shows that man needs the material as well as the spiritual, and Christ gave meaning to both aspects of our world and life.

Counseling on money matters is available from various sources

---

Waldo J. Werning is executive secretary of stewardship for the Lutheran Church—Missouri Synod in South Wisconsin. He is widely known as a speaker, author, and workshop leader.

—banks, credit agencies, insurance companies. Newspapers and magazines often offer counsel as well as educational films and materials to help families with financial planning.

Churches have a special opportunity and obligation to provide guidance to their members in money management. Some Christians have financial difficulties and are not committed to the discipline required in handling money. Some find themselves in a rather chaotic condition which grows out of a lack of planning or from poor planning. Many families are experiencing frustrations with financial problems which even second incomes do not solve. Personal desires and wants often keep far ahead of incomes.

Many marriage counselors report that money problems which are not being adequately dealt with are often at the base of family tensions and difficulties. Easy-credit buying has caused many families to obligate themselves financially far in excess of their resources. Most Christians do not adequately view money as a means for expressing their Christian faith. Recently, a New York *Times* service reported, "Recession Helping Marriages Go Broke." One couple interviewed stated, "We had a horrible case of the 'I wants.' "

Churches that provide family financial counseling will help people gain insight and new awareness of what financial resources are available, of how Christian money management requires careful attention to the total family income and total family spending (which also involves saving and giving), of the importance of counseling (especially in crisis situations), of making financial adjustments that are required from time to time, and of using the church as a ready resource. Family financial counseling is one of the most obvious needs of church families.

God's Plan for the Christian

Everything; including planning and deciding the use of possessions and money, is to be managed by the Christian in such a way that Christ is head. The Christian is God's manager and administrator, and he or she has a responsibility in all actions to witness to his or her Christian faith, to "declare the wonderful deeds of him who has called you out of darkness into his marvelous light" (1 Pet. 2:9, rsv).

Managing our lives and possessions comes into focus when we are reminded: "Therefore if any man be in Christ, he is a new creature: old things are passed away; behold, all things are become new" (2 Cor. 5:17). Through the miracle of God's grace, we become new creatures and gain a new set of values and a new outlook on life, including the handling of our money. The world is filled with people who do not know who they are and what to do with the things they have, but Christians are released from slavery to possessions as they find newness and renewal through Jesus by the forgiveness of sins.

Christianity is all about how sin can be removed from lives through faith in Jesus. Sin is a very real part of human experience; so repentance should also be a living experience, followed by forgiveness which washes away our guilt in the blood of Christ. As a response to God's grace, Christians express their faith in good management of money and are people of principle, honesty, and integrity as they fulfill their purpose in life. Christians should look to the unprecedented wealth of even average people as a test of faith and a spiritual responsibility, remembering their accountability as managers for God.

God's plan includes the use of income and possessions for the physical, spiritual, educational, social, and recreational needs of people. Besides supplying people with enough resources to support body and life, God has also made adequate provision for financing his work in the church. This is a revolutionary fact as families consider the use of their incomes.

Money problems and inflation have a spiritual cause and spiritual solution, as may be seen in Haggai. God told his people, "Consider your ways. You have sown much but bring in little, and he that earns wages earns wages to put them into a bag with holes (inflation). Build the house of God, and I will be glorified. You look for much, but it comes to little, and when you bring it home, I blow it away. Why? Because the Lord's house lies in waste while your concern is your own homes. I have called for a drought upon the land and upon the labor of your hands. The silver is mine, and gold is mine, says the Lord of Hosts. Consider from the twenty-fourth day of the ninth month, even from the day that the foundation of the Lord's temple is laid, from this day will I bless you" (paraphrase of Haggai 1, 2).

The people experienced inflation and money problems because they put their own affairs and homes before God and his work. When they had a change of heart and started laying the foundation of the temple, God gave them his blessing.

God said, "If you are willing and obedient, you shall eat the good of the land" (Isa. 1:19, RSV). The plan of God requires obedience to his will and obedience in faith, which the Bible makes clear.

As Christians we have three objectives in spending our money: God's glory, our own needs, and the needs of others. The order of priority between God and man is precise. God says, "No other gods before me . . . Love God with your whole self . . . Love your neighbor as yourself . . . Seek first the kingdom of God." God's plan is that Christians give to the Lord first and plan sensibly and reasonably the use of all their income and possessions by good management. Proper values will also be adopted in using money to provide for learning and fun and for expanding the horizons of life beyond mere existence.

Paul introduced giving as a feature of weekly worship to the churches of Galatia and Corinth (1 Cor. 16:2). Offerings are an expression of our faith in Jesus and our love for him, a joyful part of worship (Ps. 96:7-8). No better system has been devised than regularly taking out of each dollar a certain definite percentage and putting it aside for church and charitable purposes.

Establish and Clarify Values

Economic decisions are made on the basis of one's philosophy of life. People spend according to their attitudes and spiritual values. Attitudes and values dictate the standard of life which a person demands, and they determine how money is spent—for good or evil.

The temptation is to allow the values of our social group to override the values of our Christian faith. Determining family values is not easy as husband and wife bring their own sets of values to the marriage and both individually and as a unit are influenced by cultural and traditional factors.

Parents are tempted to try to inculcate adult values upon the young by moralizing or simply by demanding that their own values be transferred to them. Sharing values works best when there is a consistency about what constitutes "desirable" values. It should be recognized that while parents offer one set of "shoulds" and "should nots," the church may suggest another, while the peer group offers a third set of values, popular magazines and TV another, the school yet another, and the president and Congress of the United States still one more set of values. Too often the important choices in life are made on the basis of peer pressure, or the power of propaganda, or the unthinking submission to authority.

Understanding and examining one's motives and reasons are an important part of achieving worthy values. Money has awesome power to bless or curse. One's financial record or bank account only tells a small part about that person. A person is rich according to what he or she is and according to his or her values, not according to what he or she has. The true value of money lies not in its possession but in its use.

Wrong spiritual values cause confusion, anxiety, and fear and result in improperly earning and handling money. True Christian values will help one establish right goals and spend money in a Christian manner.

Greed and covetousness cause human values to deteriorate and cause persons to place things above human worth. John D. Rockefeller was once asked how you can make a man happy, and he answered, "By giving him just a little bit more." Forty percent of what Americans own is not essential to physical well-being and consists of optional or near-luxury items. Alexander Solzhenitsyn on June 30, 1975, in Washington, D. C., said: "Something which is incomprehensible to the human mind is the West's fantastic greed for profit for gain which goes far beyond all reason, all limitations, good conscience." Jesus said, "Beware of covetousness, for a man's life does not consist of an abundance of things which he possesses." Covetousness and greed cause various problems—inflation, unmanageable debts, and family arguments.

Getting more money is not always the solution to financial solvency (Eccles. 5:10). The true value of anything depends, not upon a price tag, but upon the extent to which it can satisfy our desires and fulfill life's necessities. The worth of anything is determined by the amount of the assistance or satisfaction that it gives. People should not needlessly deprive themselves of helpful things that contribute to their usefulness to God and to others, or that might add to their comfort, enjoyment, and broaden their knowledge. It is deplorable to spend what should have been saved; it is equally bad to save what should have been carefully spent.

The hope for establishing and clarifying proper values will depend upon avoiding speculative philosophies, naturalistic ethics, relativism, idealism, and situational ethics. Surrounded by a bewildering array of alternatives, Christians should analyze their financial habits on the basis of biblical and Christian values. Values based on scriptural standards should mold our spending patterns. Christian faith forms and shapes a person's values, which determine goals and behaviors.

Factors in Money Management

There are certain basic things one needs to understand and calculate in order to be a good money manager. A person needs to:

1. Know what he owns
2. Know what he owes
3. Know what his total income is
4. Know where his money goes by maintaining an accurate record and by developing a spending guide
5. Learn to live on his income (this means that he learns to say no consistently when it is necessary)
6. Know the cost of credit
7. Recognize what are essentials and nonessentials in spending money (these are to be separated into *fixed* and *flexible* expenses)
8. Make definite plans for family financial management and security (including safety)
9. Make effective disposition of all possessions at the time of death by writing a Christian will
10. Watch waste, a great factor in administration of businesses, factories, government departments, hospitals, and *homes*

Genuine Christian standards need to be established to avoid

foolish waste and unnecessary expenditures of all that God has given us. Unnecessary wear and tear on various items both inside and outside the house and on clothing is waste of money. Every member of the family needs to be conscious of the ways in which he or she contributes to the waste of family income through careless or thoughtless treatment of property, income, or food and through poor planning.

A general guide for the Christian use of money would involve the following categories of expenditures:

1. Support of the total work of the church at home or abroad
2. Living needs (food, clothing, shelter, taxes, medical care, transportation, repairs, insurance)
3. Life improvement (vacation, education, books, hobbies, recreation)
4. Economic security (life insurance, bank account, investments, and savings)
5. Danger–keep out (excesses, most luxuries, gambling, anything unwholesome)

Families should write up a list of their important goals: (1) things they need and want soon—a new suit or dress, an automatic washer, larger church offerings, a fund for recreation, larger savings for retirement; (2) things they want during the next year—getting old bills paid, provision for medical care, a better vacation; (3) things they want in the future—a new car, larger savings, a home of their own or a better home.

A portion of the income should be invested in savings. Principles of saving are taught in the Scriptures: the example of the wisdom of the ant storing up for future need (Prov. 6:6–8; 30:24–25); the foolish spend unwisely (Prov. 21:20); avoid risky investments and "get-rich-quick" schemes (Prov. 21:5; 28:20, 22); saving is not to be done on the basis of lack of faith or impure motives or out of anxiety (Luke 12:13–24; 1 Tim. 6:6–10).

False values create situations in which the family is saddled with debts that deprive them of the real necessities of life. Far too many paychecks are spent on frills and luxuries before providing for necessities. Many do not understand that the high cost of finance tends to cause one to waste income on interest payments instead of using income to supply basic needs.

Credit and borrowing are justified to provide funds not otherwise available when sickness, death, unemployment, or some large purchase that is deemed necessary is required. Borrowing is not justified in order to obtain luxuries, postpone a necessary reduction in one's standard of living, provide cultural frills, or indulge in speculation. Financial stability is weakened when credit is used. Keep in mind these rules for credit: (1) Borrow the least you need, not the most you can get. (2) Make the largest monthly payments you can, not the smallest the creditor will permit. (3) Don't borrow far in advance of an actual need. (4) Borrow from the lowest source, which may not be the handiest or quickest. (5) Know the true rate of interest.

FAMILY DYNAMICS

Money management is a family affair. If the family hopes to have a wholesome experience in handling their income, they should talk together about their past use of money without criticizing one another and should make plans for the present. Handling money involves a person in an endless chain of relationships with other people, starting in the family itself. Love and respect for God show themselves in respect for the rights of our fellow-men. Thus Christian integrity is to be evident in family relationships and dealing with one another in money matters.

Family Decisions

Although responsibility for major policy decisions in the use of money may rest ultimately with the parents, financial planning is best worked out by the family as a unit, all members participating according to their ability and need. Together the family should evaluate the needs and pressures they face and then apply sound Christian principles in planning their spending. In the process, each member of the family learns self-denial for the good of the family and ultimately for themselves. Thus it becomes necessary to evaluate the objectives and goals of the family and of each member.

Husbands and wives should privately discuss first what each wants and needs, and then they should consult with the children who are old enough to understand their views. The entire family must be made aware of fixed and committed expenses. Each family member should receive a proper share of family income and not be denied necessary funds when other members receive adequate funds.

We cannot develop an average budget for a family because money values and needs change as families change. The beginning family requires heavy purchases of durable goods while the income is relatively small but rising. The expanding family needs larger living quarters and encounters expanding food expenses, medical bills, clothing costs, car ownership, life insurance coverage, and school expenses. The contracting family, which grows steadily smaller until no children remain, may find peak spending power, where the family spends a smaller proportion of its income on fixed expenses and relies less and less on installment credit. The elderly couple faces a completely new situation, depending upon the amount of savings and investments they have acquired.

Children's Stewardship

Children should have an opportunity to learn effective use of money at an early age, realizing that possession of money necessitates choices—whether to save or spend and on what to spend. Children who learn good stewardship of money in the years of dependency will show more responsibility when they become independent. At an early age they should learn to take care of themselves and their possessions as a trust from God and to protect property and to respect the rights of other individuals. They should learn to share gladly their gifts and abilities and to be aware of and to meet the needs of others. Progressively they should participate in planning with the family in the Christian use of money, abilities, and possessions.

Children should be given allowances both because they have needs to be met and because they must learn how to handle money. They need to learn the difference between short-term and long-term objectives and how to evaluate the many different items for which they can spend their incomes. The amount of money that children receive should be related to their needs and maturity.

Even though parents can afford to give everything to their children, they should not do so, for children need to learn some degree of independence and gain a sense of personal achievement. Allowances should not be given as rewards or as payment for doing chores, nor should they be withheld for poor grades in school, bad behavior, or a similar reason. Children should seek to do commendable work at home and school because of the responsibility involved. One is not paid for doing or being good, nor can money purchase the affection or approval of others. Work is a given, a fact of life, and there is no such thing as "no work" on the part of any healthy family member.

Careful thought should be given to financial arrangements with children because they become conditioned to a pattern of events which they expect to continue and which creates certain behavior habits. Children who are conditioned to gratification expect things to be acquired without effort on their part by making a demand or creating a "scene." Children need a sense and dignity of achievement, but too much pressure for achievement beyond ability puts too much strain on them, which has a destructive effect and causes anxiety, tension, and aggressive behavior.

Teens have trouble spending wisely. The Rand Youth Poll reported in *Youth Today* that 38 percent say they buy ridiculous products to satisfy their egos and frustrations, that two-thirds think their friends are making foolish purchases, and that teenage savings are short term.

As children and youth earn money, they can be helped to set up spending plans and records of their own which are simple at first and then expanded to suit their growing earning power. Setting financial priorities, including offerings to our Savior, should be learned.

Parents need to set clearly defined standards and limits. Properly administered, these guides are a sign of loving children enough to care about their well-being by defining limits and holding to them, including handling money. All should realize that the use of money is a revealing index to their character and to their heart's attitude and commitment to Christ.

PRINCIPLES OF MONEY MANAGEMENT

Planning for spending money (budgeting) helps select a standard of living within one's income. A suitable spending guide encourages responsible choices, frees rather than confines, and stimulates rather than depresses. It rewards good thinking and wise action and aids in attaining important goals. Good planning tends to eliminate family arguments about finances.

The guiding principle of a budget is not to record expenses but to know and control them. Good financial planning will allow the family to gain a better standard of living at the same cost.

Poorly made decisions produce confusion, guilt, and feelings of helplessness. Proper decisions depend upon adequate information, deciding what is important, understanding the rewards for balanced thinking and planning, and realizing that the quality of our lives is affected.

Effective financial decisions are based upon a number of principles:

1. Get the facts. Probe and question in a way that values will be clarified. Determine what is important, what is needed, and what is available.

2. Define the goal. Maintain financial stability, make maximum use of total income and each dollar, understand all alternatives, write your own goals, and establish your own budget. Seek to use all resources according to God's plan and purpose. Understand your motives for spending. Look at your finances in God's perspective, and set a goal of a specific percentage for the Lord's work *first.*

3. Establish priorities. Decide what shall be achieved now and what later. Rank the matters of importance now as they should be reflected in the actual spending guide. Don't confuse your priorities and miss God's plan for your life.

4. Develop a plan. Choice is between effective and ineffective management. Decide how money is to be used on a monthly basis in the context of the annual budget.

5. Keep adequate records. Simply, list the annual income, total fixed expenses, the balance available for variable expenses, and the amount you have left.

6. *Allow for revision.* By watching carefully the financial records as they are kept, the plan can be kept flexible in order to make revisions. Learn self-discipline.

Decision Making and Mechanics to Maintain Accurate Records

The simplest directions for keeping a record of family expenses involve these steps:

1. Jot down item by item how you spent your income in the past months, and then decide whether you really want to spend that much on these items.

2. Draw up a list of your most important goals: church offerings, a possession or replacement of something worn out, savings, old debts, education for children, and so on.

3. Make up a monthly budget for the next year that cuts down on items where savings can be made and boosts spending for things you really want.

4. Keep a day-by-day record of every penny you spend. At the end of each month compare what you have actually spent on each item with what was budgeted.

Techniques for money management need not be difficult or overly time consuming. Find an easy-to-manage system for keeping account of and improving your family's financial situation.

Train Families in Financial Planning

Most of the training of people in financial planning and budgeting is done on a crisis basis by banks or loan agencies. Good counseling should be preventive and actually prepare families for facing life on a sound financial basis. The church should be prepared to help young families before financial crises threaten their marriage or happiness and to help families plan their estates and build retirement programs.

Several approaches should be considered in assisting couples and families to be fiscally responsible:

Pastors should consider advising for effective Christian money management in premarital counseling sessions. The pastor might suggest that the couple review a filmstrip on financial planning and then counsel with them regarding this matter.

Practical assistance might be given in a worship service by a qualified layman and the pastor through a study of a "Christian Money Management Guide" provided to all members. The members should be given both the motivation and the practical assistance to budget their incomes according to Christian priorities.

Selected couples who have the potential to teach classes or counsel people might participate in a group study. The schedule could be for six weeks, meeting once a week for one to one and one-half hours. Capable laymen and qualified specialists with deep Christian commitment should provide assistance in Christian stewardship of income, family budgeting, costs of banking and borrowing, real estate investments, insurance, educational costs, wills, annuities, and so on. Both husband and wife should know their assets and liabilities.

A program of family money management is a vital service for any parish that wishes to minister to its families in a very important aspect of life.

The books and materials listed below will provide basic resources for the Christian family money management program:

Ford, George L. *All the Money You Need*. Waco, Tex.: Word Books, 1976.
Spear, Michael L. *A Complete Guide to the Christian's Budget*. Nashville: Broadman Press, 1975. Provides help for budgeting and money management in such areas as attitude, why, how, debts, credit, giving, teaching children, insurance, estate planning, saving, investment, and careful planning.
Werning, Waldo J. *Where Does the Money Go?* Winona Lake, Ind.: Light and Life Press, 1972.

The following materials are available from Louis Neibauer Company, Benson East, Township Line and Old York Road, Jenkintown, Pennsylvania 19046.

Growing in Personal and Family Stewardship Manual supplies the purpose, goals, method, plan, and calendar for the Christian Family Money Management Program. This guide will assist church leaders as they plan a program designed to reach toward faithful and careful handling of possessions and incomes.

Christian Family Money Management and Financial Planning (budget book, 35¢, 24 pages) helps Christian families plan for organized spending, giving, and saving.

Family Spending Guide (4 pages, 8½-by-11-inches) is an easy-to-follow financial guide which shows the principles of family money management and how to achieve financial goals. May be used as a summary form of a budget.

Focus on Your Family's Future (3¢) presents thought-provoking questions to the family in regard to specific plans for future financial needs.

A Family Covenant Commitment (2¢) is a specially designed certificate bearing scriptural quotations for a family commitment for the Christian use of income and all resources.

Why Money? (12 pages, 10¢) is a booklet that provides a biblical basis for handling and using money. Good for use in group meetings or in home visits.

Family Money Management Counseling Kit, available from the National Consumer Finance Association, 1000 16th St., N.W., Washington, D.C. 20036. Especially helpful is the booklet *Money and Your Marriage* which treats "values in marriage, getting the most out of your financial resources, having your family, earning extra income, your financial security, and managing your marriage." Also available is a Teacher's Kit, a one-week advanced teaching unit on consumer credit, which includes the teacher's materials and the student's materials.

Money Management Library, available from Household Finance Corporation, Presidential Plaza, Chicago, Ill. 60601. Provides excellent resources through a series of books and a teacher's guide. The complete set is available for $3.50. Each book separately costs 35¢.

Reaching Your Financial Goals; It's Your Credit—Manage It Wisely; Children's Spending, Your Food Dollar; Your Housing Dollar; Your Home Furnishings Dollar; Your Equipment Dollar; Your Shopping Dollar; Your Automobile Dollar; Your Health and Recreation Dollar; Your Savings and Investment Dollar; Your Guide for Teaching Money Management.
Available also is a tract entitled *Money Talks, or You've Got to Have a Plan, Man!* which provides six simple steps for making financial plans and establishing a budget.

6.

Leisure, Vacations, and the Family

William D. Gwinn

The family unit has been fragmented so consistently in our United States culture that a close-knit family is becoming an increasingly rare phenomenon. With school in session much of the day, plus club activities and intramural or interscholastic sports, musical and drama events, and the time required to get to and from school, family time is reduced sharply. Many families do not eat breakfast together, and virtually none eat lunch together, leaving only dinner as a possible time for family sharing and fellowship.

The increasing number of working mothers, whether out of desire or necessity, has deprived countless children of the availability of a mother to listen, console, encourage, or correct on children's arrival home from school. The concerted effort of various forces in our society to downgrade marriage, motherhood, and even the family as a valid basis of the creative order has done major damage to the whole concept of the family. The rapidly increasing acceptability of divorce as an easy solution to tension in marriage has placed into serious jeopardy couples who previously worked hard to resolve differences.

Televisions, radios, stereos, and telephones, without disciplined

William D. Gwinn is executive director of Mount Hermon Christian Conference Center, Mount Hermon, California. He is also president of Christian Camping International.

control, have intruded seriously upon whatever time there may have been otherwise for the family to communicate about homework, dad's vocation, current events, and so on.

Regular family devotional times are the exception rather than the rule even in the most well-intentioned Christian homes.

Even the local church has clouded its own biblicalness by failing to acknowledge the centrality of the family as God's basic unit for evangelism, nurture, and outreach to a community. It is true, ironically, that the local church may be the most serious violator in fragmenting the family.

Many pastors, in the course of being the legitimate shepherd of a flock, assume the role of spiritual priest for the family, usurping this God-established role from the father. Fortunately, more and more pastors are gearing their ministry around discipling men who can in turn lead their families, even to the point of enabling whole families to help families without a Christian father or any father at all.

Local churches are programmed so heavily that it is all too rare to find a church which leaves more than one night a week, if that, for the family to be a complete unit together, let alone share their home with others. Various activities, however good they may be, need the scissor treatment in favor of higher priorities. Even pastoral staffs and church officers need relief from attendance at some events so their own families can stay healthy. We need to become more able to relax in seeing the local church dark some nights in favor of lighted homes.

Departmentalization, a valuable device when held in check, has become the framework for the life of many local churches, not just the Sunday school. Whether prompted by space problems or by educational philosophy, primary and junior churches have been formed so that the family, in so-called family-centered churches, does not even sit together for worship. Even such family members as may be physically present within the same sanctuary do not sit together, thus losing a crucial "check and balance" value and often creating a side-room or balcony disturbance problem. Preaching as I do in dozens of churches each year, I am always pleased to find a church (and they are rare) in which families sit together and to find a service prepared with the entire family in mind. It is dramatic to note the difference in atmosphere when families sit together.

The home, instead of being the center for witness, has become just a rest-and-repair center. As valuable as various programs of visitation have been, the Bible has far more to say about the ministry of hospitality than it does about visitation, other than of the widowed, elderly, and afflicted. How much better to invite a person, couple, or family into *our* home at *their* convenience than for us to intrude *their* castle at *our* convenience. Few encounters are more memorable than those we have with friends, new or old, in our home or in theirs. Home Bible studies, which are becoming more and more prevalent, are highly effective, but there is also great need for the natural life-on-life contact in meal fellowship, conversation, the fun of playing together, and hopefully praying together. If we have healthy homes, we need to put them on display. If we do not, opening our homes will quickly reveal our weak spots so we can go to work on them.

LEISURE

Every individual needs to call "time out" along the way to relax, repair, and recoup. This may be accomplished through sports, music, painting the house, reading, photography, gardening, a meal out with spouse, special outing with each of your children, exercise programs, an extra nap, make-it-yourself hobbies of various kinds, or a host of other activities.

One of the most effective means of leisure is for the family to do things together—helping others, yard or house chores, touring a factory near your home, playing games, enjoying picnics with another family, having another family or friends of your children into your home. There is great value in activities of involvement rather than just spectator activities, as legitimate as the latter may be when in balance.

In any case, it is crucial for most of us to reduce our pace so we can maintain perspective on life. The poem "Slow Me Down, Lord" says it well:

Slow me down, Lord. Ease the pounding of my heart by the quieting of my mind.

Steady my hurried pace with a vision of the eternal reach of time.

Give me, amid the confusion of the day, the calmness of the everlasting hills.

Break the tensions of my nerves and muscles with the soothing music of the singing streams that live in my memory. Help me to know the magical, restoring power of sleep.

Teach me the art of taking minute vacations—of slowing down to look at a flower, to chat with a friend, to pat a dog, to read a few lines from a good book.

Slow me down, Lord, and inspire me to send my roots deep into the soul of life's enduring values that I may grow toward the stars of my greater destiny.

Author Unknown

If nothing else, we can all take "minute vacations." We can at least stop long enough to look at a flower, enjoy a sunrise or sunset, marvel at the moon and the stars, pet a dog, visit with a child or an elderly passer-by.

As urgent as is the need to make Christ known, there is no justification for "workaholics" in the kingdom of God. Many are so obsessed, whatever their motivation, with the need for activity that they have little or no opportunity to enjoy life and to become the healthy, whole, well-rounded people who will be attractive to non-Christians. "Burning the candle at both ends" is not a wise or disciplined spiritual exercise, however piously defended. *Private* leisure moments are perhaps even more crucial than group ones, but hobbies and diversions which are strictly solitary in nature can tend to erode family unity to a major degree. They need to be shared in some way.

VACATIONS

As valuable as days off and "minute vacations" can be, there is a crucial need for *concentrated* periods of time when families can get away from the usual routine and enjoy new places, new people, and new experiences. A vacation for a family is a time when everyone can do together things which are not normally possible with the day-to-day demands of pressured schedules and responsibilities. These diversions will express themselves in different ways with different families.

Whereas my work has been highly demanding in the summer, as a family we have faithfully taken time, even when we haven't had it, during the winter, sometimes taking the children out of school, to have special outings as a family. I only wish there could have been more such times and that they could have been longer. So soon our children are gone, as depicted in the songs "Sunrise, Sunset" from *Fiddler on the Roof* and "Turn Around." Whatever could have been more important than the cherished memories of shared travel and adventure together?

The board of directors of Mount Hermon Christian Conference Center near San Francisco, where I have served since 1957, initiated a special family vacation leave this past summer, in a desire to enable my wife and me to travel with our four children before they "leave the nest" since our oldest is twenty-one. Though we have done many special things together through the years, extended travel opportunities have never been possible, and especially not in the summer.

We traveled 9600 miles around the western United States in a rented motor home for ten weeks. It was an experience unequaled in my lifetime in spite of an extensive six-week, eleven-thousand-mile trip my own family of eight took the summer of 1939 when I had my tenth birthday.

We were able to visit old friends, churches of several denominations and styles of worship and architecture, sister camps, other countries (Canada and Mexico), experience other cultures and life-styles, see new places, have a host of new adventures, and enjoy several national parks (the Grand Tetons were tops with us!) and other scenic spots (Butchart Gardens were tough to beat). We backpacked down into the Grand Canyon to the Colorado River, bicycled around the rim of the canyon and many other places throughout the trip, water-skied, played golf and tennis, swam in cold lakes and warm pools, rode horses through unsurpassed Colorado scenery, paddled canoes, threw Frisbees galore, picked wild blackberries, slept out under the stars many nights, stayed on a dairy farm, saw a junior rodeo in Denton, Texas, dropped in on the Josephine County Fair in Oregon, and toured the Air Force Academy (the dishwashing department of which is larger than Mount Hermon's entire kitchen). We marveled at God's creative power and artistry expressed in so many ways—cloud formations, rainbows, sunsets, sunrises, moon and star shows, wildflowers, birds (including our first osprey, along the Rogue River), animals (including our first moose, in Yellowstone), rivers and lakes, rock outcroppings, and majestic mountains.

We read, conversed, relaxed, recreated, and toured to our heart's content. We struggled with interpersonal relationships aggravated by crises without number and by the clash of six wills cooped up in one motor home. We learned much about love and forgiveness and how to adjust to one another, more than we'd ever faced at home. We learned so much from and about each other. I had prayed it would be an educational experience rather than a time of self-indulgence, and God answered my prayers. The trip's chief characteristic was limitless "teachable moments."

Never before had we faced and solved so much in so short a time—cranberry juice on the carpet, boiling tea on a leg, a flash-bulb burn in the Carlsbad Caverns (the camera itself was a crisis to be dealt with, though all are enjoying the results), burned-out pilot lights, three flat tires in Texas in forty-eight hours, transmission problems at Tahoe far from mechanical help, carburetion headaches nearly half the trip in spite of four garage stops, varied other mechanical breakdowns (we learned to use tools and fix things we never had before), an unstoppable nosebleed, a stubborn ear infection, two near-fractures, maintaining a modicum of modesty in intimate, tight quarters (and learning to relax with the intimacy), wrestling a watermelon amid limited refrigeration space, meeting a school bus on a narrow one-lane mountain pass, being awakened by police and rangers in the wee hours in spite of previous permission, making beds without elbow room, dropping the soap in the tiny shower, finding the toilet won't flush anymore and no pumping station for miles, getting by with a broken dining table for several days, handling laundry with minimum storage and far-away laundromats, failing to switch gas tanks properly and being stranded in thick traffic for ninety minutes outside Yellowstone National Park, fighting a single fly or mosquito against brown walls, and *many* more. We always

faced the crisis better if we'd had some time with God. It was
a great help to have strategic memory verses mounted on the
wall the last part of the trip to remind us all what the demands
of Scripture were and where the power comes from to heed
them. We also found it infinitely true that the family who prays
together stays together. We wouldn't have if we hadn't!

The opportunity to encourage various relatives and friends
along the way and to share Christ with various ones to whom
God led us kept us involved in a life laboratory of giving ourselves to others. One of the most dramatic of these opportunities
was the privilege to spend ninety minutes with a former Seattle
high-school classmate who, though still claiming innocence, is
the convicted killer/kidnaper of Adolph Coors III. I was his first
visitor in his fourteen years in the Colorado State Prison! We had
a good visit. He was very warm and responsive. I pray that the
seed sown will bear fruit.

To bounce along (literally) over the ever-changing landscape
accompanied on the motor home's eight-track stereo by John
Peterson's and Don Wyrtzen's new patriotic and prayerful
musical *I Love America* gave us a bicentennial flavor hard to
improve upon. Listening each week to tapes of Mount Hermon's
Sunday worship service and Saturday evening concerts kept us
plugged into the blessing of Mount Hermon without being
operationally involved and aided substantially in the spiritual diet
of our journey. Singing together as a family with tapes and books
was a special delight. The chorus "Thou Art Worthy" based on
Revelation 4:4 became our theme song as we saw so much of
what God had created.

Whereas we were privileged as few are to make a trip like
this, most families who have summer vacations could do the same
and more, spread over several years. We all agreed it would be
better to space it out. "Where" and "what" is less important than
"that" time is taken for special experiences which will give
breadth and depth to life, as well as lifelong memories. If we had
waited until we could afford it, we would never have done it.
We simply lowered all else on the priority schedule and gave it
first place.

Unquestionably the greatest value of vacations is "clearing

the cobwebs," taking a fresh look at life—its purpose and your goals—in a new and different environment. But also of great value is the opportunity to chisel rough edges from another (and parents come in for their share). The most crucial ingredients of life for any human being to survive happily—acceptance, recognition, and self-worth—can all be infused in steady amounts in a vacation atmosphere. Respecting another's viewpoint, complimenting him or her for an expression or act, inviting interaction from the more reserved ones through good questions, and apologizing and forgiving especially after hard encounters all go far toward building up one another. We learned early in our trip that no one could survive in an atmosphere filled with the "put-downs" so common in routine family life, but we needed constantly to watch our stance toward one another. We could not afford to be careless in this when each day was full of so much pressure. It finally dawned on us it shouldn't happen at home either, unless carefully pondered so as to be "speaking the truth in love."

It has been my observation through twenty-five years of counseling young people that few concerns have made them more bitter toward their parents or their parents' jobs or churches or other Christian involvements than the failure of many parents to give vacation experiences high priority each year. There is no way to justify the oft-heard statement, "We haven't had a vacation, at least away from here, for nearly ten years now." That's dedication, all right, but to the wrong thing.

A Specialized Kind of Vacation

Having served at Mount Hermon Christian Conference Center for eighteen years in youth and family camping and as president of Christian Camping International I feel that families need to be aware of the specialized kinds of vacations offered by Christian camps and conferences. Christian camping has become to the church in the past two decades what the Sunday school was in the first half of this century, now becoming an extension of the Sunday school away from the church plant. I use the term *camping* here in its broadest sense to cover both wilderness and facility experiences, both activity-centered and meeting-centered programming, both counselor-centered and speaker-centered approaches, both camps and conferences.

Christian educators have come to believe that the *concentrated* experience which camping allows for a weekend, a week, or longer provides a *laboratory* in the lordship of Christ second only to the Christian home (or motor home!). Virtually every denomination and local church which is effectively touching lives for Christ employs camping in some major way, either for evangelism or nurture or both. Most major missionary agencies, both in the United States and in other countries, are building or renting facilities where they can have longer blocks of time in a more lifelike environment with the people they are seeking to reach or train. Young Life, Youth for Christ, Campus Crusade, Inter-Varsity Christian Fellowship, the Navigators, and the Salvation Army all build much of what they do around camping opportunities. The Evangelical Alliance Mission and Overseas Crusades have both placed great emphasis on camping to accomplish their goals, as have many others. Today CCI, a worldwide affiliation of evangelical camps, has member camps in fifty countries. This is a phenomenal story of expanded ministry just in the last decade.

Family camping, our specialty at Mount Hermon, has become more and more popular as a means of both evangelism and nurture. We seek to provide a total re-creational program for the family—spiritually, physically, socially, and mentally. Some opportunities are provided by age groups with peers, but most programming is built around family togetherness, from making beds to Bible reading, to sand sculpture at the Santa Cruz beach, to singing and worshiping together around the campfire, to roasting and eating "smores" over a fire of coals, to being stimulated in the relevance of God's Word for family life by top resource people. Everything is programmed to increase family communication and comfortableness with one another. Every effort is made to remove masks and to encourage transparency, first with Christ and then with one another.

Youth and children's camping has retained its popularity because "kids too need a vacation." And it is extremely valuable to have the supporting influence of a counselor of near age who reinforces what has been emphasized at home or by a pastor for months or years. The most successful youth camps are simulated family experiences in staffing and programming philosophy, and the goal is to send each person back into his or her family to be more supportive, cooperative, and contributory to the welfare of other family members, and as well to the church "family," all in the power of the Spirit rather than the flesh.

With a longer unpressured time to get an audience for the gospel, and in a relational atmosphere of new adventure, acceptance, and accomplishment, many open their hearts to receive Christ. The seed sown by faithful parents, Sunday school teachers, pastors, youth workers, or other friends takes root and begins to bear fruit. Children from broken homes or homes lacking acceptance and love are helped significantly in a happy camp setting. (Camping is one of the best family substitutes available.) With daily study in the Scriptures, and time to deal with questions and doubts in an atmosphere of love and patience, Christians grow rapidly and begin to form strong, abiding life-goals.

Many families rotate their vacations by taking an extended trip one year and then staying in a camp for a full week, often closer to home, another year, believing that the combination of a fun opportunity and supplementary spiritual input is too valuable to pass by. And many families budget to send their children to camp another week in addition to a family week because of the special values each provides.

Specialized work, service, and wilderness camps, pastors/ Christian writers/church music/and leadership training conferences, couples conferences (no children allowed), single adults conferences, senior citizens midweeks, and conferences of vocational groupings are some of the new opportunities being provided by various camps. Christian camps have become an extremely valuable tool to the church. More are being built, but existing ones continue to grow and maintain a high occupancy, not only in the summer but now year-round in many areas.

Vacations take many forms, but every person and every family need them. Our Lord and his disciples did, and so do we the more, as life accelerates and becomes more complicated.

I am so grateful to have been able this summer to practice

what we at Mount Hermon preach, that all families need a change of pace and place, whether at a camp or elsewhere.

I am confident the entire body of Christ would be stronger and healthier if we would pause long enough to get a good fresh look, at least annually, at our goals and values, as well as at our methods of achieving them.

As valuable and necessary as personal vacations and vacations as couples are, do not forget the children. We all need this kind of qualitative and quantitative experience together. We need to nourish our family's health, for we need their closeness and support, and they ours, to be maximally effective in our witness for Christ in the world.

The pressures of materialism will be offset when you return from vacations. Home never looks so good! We shall be much slower to take many things for granted again. We will seek even more to have our house be a true home, to be lived in, enjoyed, and shared—a place to be cared for to be sure, but not a neurotic museum as houses are to many people.

Somebody needs to start putting the family back together again! We need some examples to launch a contagion in our culture that will reawaken in others a holy regard for the way God put it all together in the first place. As for me and my house, we are going *his* route. We refuse to let "the world around us squeeze us into *its* mold." (Rom. 12:1, 2, Phillips).

*The Family
and Outside Pressures*

7.

The Family in Today's World

Mark Hatfield

A recent issue of *Newsweek* magazine related the story of the Caruso family in California. The father, Joe Caruso, much like many other American fathers, is a conscientious worker and is locally active in politics and in the community theater. He attends church regularly, and he prays before meals. But all is not well with the Caruso family. Joe's three daughters haven't chosen his life-style. Although still teenagers, the two oldest daughters have their own apartment. The two younger ones have experimented with drugs. One ran away from home at sixteen. Joe's fifteen-year-old daughter left home and was later arrested for participating in armed robbery. Joe and his wife subsequently have attended classes in parenting.

Researchers are learning that Joe's problems are not uncommon in our changing society. They, for that matter, are not that uncommon among church families today. They are often the result of confused values; and as various cultural forces bear down upon the child, he or she must make early choices about values. Without considerable support from the family, a child's values naturally reflect the dominant influences upon him or her. Even when parents seek to guide children in developing values, they

---

Mark Hatfield is the United States Senator from Oregon. He is the author of *Conflict and Conscience* and *Between a Rock and a Hard Place.*

often find that the children's choices are not what they as parents had hoped for.

The independence of adolescence results in natural challenges to almost all the accepted values in the parents' lives, and I believe this is true in nearly all facets of life. I find that my fifteen-year-old son has become very conservative in his political thinking. He's obviously challenging part of his parenthood. Challenges differ widely, reflecting different perspectives. For instance, children often seem more concerned with introspective relational matters than with the economics of living, matters which are very important to their parents.

In thinking about the family in today's world, one is forced to recognize both the complexity of the issue and certain assumptions in relation to the family. One assumption is that the concept of the family must include some consideration of the persons not in nuclear family situations. For instance, in the 1920s 50 percent of the families in our nation included at least one extra adult. Today that percentage has been reduced to less than 5 percent as we shunt grandparents, aunts, uncles, and others off to lonely existences in retirement homes, nursing homes, and often less-than-adequate apartments.

Another assumption is that the family is an important basic element in our society. A third assumption is that we concur that God has an interest in family development and that the Scriptures have clear instructions regarding family life and family responsibilities.

The secular world is expressing an interest in the condition of the family, and family-support programs further confirm the importance of the family. A recent introduction in the United States Senate of a bill entitled "Family and Household Research Act of 1975" was accompanied by a statement referring to findings by the Senate Subcommittee on Children and Youth that families are the most vital and fundamental institutions of this nation and that families are experiencing numerous difficulties and pressures in an increasingly complex, technological society. (As a point of information, the purpose of the bill is simply to broaden the knowledge of the pressures on families.)

There are also a number of significant studies, one of which was made by Uri Bronfenbrenner, social psychologist at Cornell University. He cites those outside forces which often result in overwhelming loneliness and the loss of a sense of community. Such things as occupational mobility and the breakdown of neighborhoods result in lonely privacy. Our suburbs become only bedroom communities as residential and business areas are separated and school districts are consolidated. Families are physically divided as each age-level develops its own social activities and as childcare is left to those outside the family. Education has become the job of the schools. Religion has become the task of the church. Care for the elderly and the infirm has been assumed to an even greater degree by the state. Even athletic experiences are "jobbed out" to others such as the Little League and professional spectator sports. Automation, which we have often discussed, depersonalizes in production. We also find all too often that in the home our relationships are based on tasks and responsibilities rather than on love for the person. We are caught up in a type of automation mentality in the family.

The Bronfenbrenner study indicates that the reduction of the number of caring adults in families actually has had a negative effect on the socialization of American children. We need one another as relatives, neighbors, and friends in caring communities.

In light of these facts, the church of Jesus Christ today has a unique opportunity to offer society a constructive alternative to present trends of family erosion. Personal reconciliation to both God and man has been the universally accepted task of the church for ages. But as we face the loss of community and the profound impact this has upon families, we find ourselves with a new challenge which cannot be simply defined as either the need for personal redemption or the need for social action. Our challenge is to build a force in society whose power is love rather than one which loves power. A new community is the challenge.

The church, the spiritual church as representing the body of Christ, is uniquely suited to building a new community and to strengthening the existing nuclear family. Over and over, as we study the Scriptures, we read of individual commitment to one another which is born, not merely of a biological relationship, but of a spiritual kinship. Ruth and Naomi experienced a deep love for each other, akin to that of a blood relationship, unlike the present-day popularization of mother-in-law/daughter-in-law relationships. David and Jonathan are remembered for their love for each other in the face of the wrath of Jonathan's father, Saul. The disciples experienced a relationship with Jesus which was closer than that of a biological family.

Jesus said, "Who is my mother? and who are my brothers? Whoever does the will of my Father in heaven is my brother and sister and mother." The early church described throughout the New Testament exhibited those characteristics which we long for today in our nuclear families: enduring love, interdependence, stability, loyalty and devotion, commitment and responsibility, security in time of crisis and old age.

The church today can help meet these needs. The church actually is an extended family. The qualities of love, preference for one another, upbuilding one another, and humility are not mutually exclusive of either the family or the church. When the church addresses the growing plight of single adults, single-parent families, and the elderly who live alone, it need not make an awkward effort to fit them into some special programs, for they are actually members of the family.

The first body of officials in the early church was organized in order to include the widows and the poor in the vital life of the church. The extended family known as the church must meet the needs of today's nuclear family also. It can give support when both parents must work. It can be compassionate in the midst of need for food and clothing and can be the mere presence of an intimate friend in time of emotional distress. It *can* provide roots or a sense of belonging, even in our mobile society.

Recently I was recalling with another person the care that we had developed during the years of the depression. We noted that even though many had very little, that very condition drew us together in the act of sharing—with family, neighbors, and friends. We experienced a real sense of interdependence and community.

I believe that the church today, the church of Jesus Christ, can re-create the sense of the supporting community. I'm sure that many of you have had the deep and wonderful experience of supporting others and being supported by others. My friendships include a group of men who are committed to one another in what we call the Fellowship. We share a commitment, not that we meet according to a regular program, but that we meet the needs of any member of that fellowship. We share ourselves and assume liability for one another. My wife belongs to a covenant group whose aim is to minister to one another. My sixteen-year-old daughter belongs to a core group. Whatever the label, whatever the name, the fact that we have created within the family of God a ministry to one another is evidence of the effective role the church can play in developing loving community. The ministry of community and the expansion of this supportive love beyond a congregation or geographic locality becomes a breeze that bears along the evangelistic message of the church.

I am talking about a dynamic, circular relationship. The body of Christ is a family. The smaller family units within the body both support the larger body and are supported by it. This concept involving unlimited liability for one another in the midst of a very uncertain world is what Christ was talking about when he said, "By this all men will know that you are my disciples, if you have love one for the other."

The goal of the church is not simply to struggle to build healthy nuclear families. The role of the church and the goal of the church must be that of a family for all the people of the body of Christ. In order to experience progress in the development of healthy family life in a changing society, we must be committed to a new style of family life consistent with the Scripture. First, we must recognize that even as the body of Christ we have become enculturated by a world which does not reflect God's values.

Family includes relationships between people which can reach beyond mere biological cause and effect. Family is a life-style to be extended inward and outward. Families are not an accident of cohabitation but a practice in relationships. Given the need for the influence of caring adults on children, the body of Christ must take the offensive in family affairs. The purpose of the family is to protect, to shape, and to draw out developing lives. Such is also the role of believers in relationship to one another. Rather than asking, "Who is raising our children?" we can today commit ourselves to the larger family of Christ, allowing this body to help shape our children.

Have you had the experience of becoming the instrumentality through which God has worked to influence the sons and daughters of other families? In turn fellow brothers and sisters in Christ influence your children and my children, perhaps in ways more effective than we as parents can. This is possible because we love and care for one another's children as part of the larger body of Christ. The church must be a force which does not retreat and look for the security of the past. We must face change. We must accept the fallen state of society as representing the corporate result of the fallen state of man. We must work as a countercultural force—loving, caring, supporting one another and our children.

We must not merely seek to reinstitute past practices, expending our energies in matters that are no longer of any great importance to the culture in which we live and which so greatly influences our families. Rather we must turn our attention to new models of care and love which speak to the changing conditions of our world. Old wineskins are not used to store new wine. In the midst of a mobile society the body of Christ must provide stability through accepting those of all ages and all backgrounds. We must reach out to our neighborhoods, bringing warmth and love and witness in the face of mistrust and alienation.

One of the great examples of such love for the larger family that I have seen was at Oral Roberts University where, built adjacent to and as an integral part of the campus, is a retirement center. In each room of that retirement center is a closed-circuit television, bringing the dynamics of the classroom into the retiree's residence. The involvement of students in labor and support services for the retirement center facilitates a great interchange between youth and old age. Rather than shunting aside, isolating the experience, the knowledge, and all the other great attributes of old age, this proximity to the campus helps create a beautiful interplay. This is but one example of what we could do within each community to be a family of God's people.

If we in God's family cannot, through the power of Christ, build bridges across generations, how can we expect the rest of society to be successful? God's family holds the key to a revolutionary model of love and hope for our society. Persons empowered by the Holy Spirit with love for one another can face the problems of life and relationships and *find* the answers. Becoming one flesh means people care for one another as they do for themselves and are drawn together by a holy love greater than their own. The church becomes a larger family with the interdependencies inherent in the concept of the body of Christ. The church needs to become a model in action, not one that is noted in the press for being torn asunder with strife and friction and schisms. And rather than fragment the family, the local church can become an agent for family development, actively caring for the forgotten and rejected who live in loneliness.

The family in America may not be well, but the cure does not lie in criticizing those in search of an answer to their innermost needs. Individuals of all ages have relational needs and look for situations where they will be met. But seeing that few families consistently meet those needs and that many other institutions and agencies do meet some needs, more people are choosing today not to become involved in permanent family relationships.

I believe that it is not the institution of the family that has failed. It is rather the individuals who have failed to practice love and discipline. An article in the *American Journal of Psychiatry* notes that the quality of marriage, family, and parenthood is determined by the quality of husbands and wives, of mothers and fathers, as people. We have expected fallen man to conform to God's plan for relationships, nurture, and support. The need exists, but the power is lacking. Into this area of need, Christians, individually and corporately, can move with hope and with a redemptive witness. Jesus said, "I came that they may have life and have it more abundantly."

Our message is one of radical revolution through Jesus Christ. If this message is first applied and if this revolution is first experienced within our individual lives, then we can infect our communities. This infectious love can spread throughout the nation. This is the new American revolution that would be greater, more earthshaking, and more world-influencing than the revolution confronting the First Continental Congress in the 1700s.

8.

The Christian's Family in Society

Ted Ward

As children of the living God, through his grace revealed in our Lord Jesus Christ, we are *"in* the world, but not *of* the world."* For the Christian family, as for the church, to be distinctive demands being different. The key task for the Christian family is to relate assertively and positively to the realities of today's world without being caught up in secular society's powerful influences. In maintaining life-long family orientations and relationships, including the crucial function of parenthood, the Christian family faces increasingly menacing forces in secular society. These forces are overcome if the family deliberately holds Christian values above secular values. The crucial values are:

1. Sanctity and commitment to the marriage relationship
2. Development of the home as a place of warmth, nurture, acceptance, and healthy stimulation
3. Learning of God and growing in grace together and individually through the Word of God and its implementation through a just, merciful, and loving life-style
4. Involvement in outreach, through the church, participating in God's redeeming work in society

---

Ted Ward is professor of curriculum research in the College of Education, Michigan State University. He is constantly in demand as a speaker, lecturer, and resource leader in the area of curriculum.

The caption on the first article in the *New Republic* of September 6, 1975, caught my eye: "The Obsolete Home." I thought, this may be the first major piece in the popular press to acknowledge that the family has been laid to rest. Home as we have known it is being written off by one after another of the opinion leaders and scientists of our time. No, it is not yet a headline story; the *New Republic* article was concerned instead with changes in housing patterns in America due largely to inflation. But the changes were not due to inflation alone, as I read in one of the secondary points in the article:

> . . . the post-war children aren't behaving like their parents. They're marrying later, divorcing more often, having fewer children and sending both men and women to work—factors that may weaken the lure of the single-family home.

Things are changing.

Several months ago I presented a brief paper at a national conference of social scientists and educators who are involved in major research and development activities in the area of moral and ethical values. In the paper I argued that the school is by no means the best bet as an institution through which to work for moral values in our society; I contended that the family is crucial, and even to assume that the church is dead is to be misled by occasional appearances. As I sat down, I expected the discussion to center on criticizing my contention that the church is still a viable instrument of human welfare. I had engaged in this debate with various colleagues in social science on many occasions. Instead, much to my surprise, the discussion immediately attacked as "archaic" and "quaint" my view that the *family* can be expected to play a significant role in values development. Didn't I know? The day of the family is over!

It was like being present at a turning point of history. Leading American and Canadian scholars were arguing that the family as we have known it is dead, for most practical purposes. Secular society is ready to abandon the family as a defunct institution. I propose three conclusions:

1. In the Christian community, the family cannot be abandoned; it is basic.

2. The Christian family is now well on the way to being distinctly different from the secular family (or from whatever substitute for the family the secular society may yet create).
3. The pressures upon this increasingly different Christian family can have certain strengthening outcomes for the church.

The first point above is essentially theological and can be supported scripturally. The second point is sociological; it can be observed by anyone who has been alert to what the "body-life" ministries, for example, are helping Christian families to become. The third point is admittedly speculative, but I would support it on historical grounds. Even as the Jerusalem church through persecution was scattered and thus became an even more world-impacting reality, the whole history of the church reminds us that Christ is glorified and the church grows through adversity. I am not at all pessimistic.

Scientists have two different ways to respond to social trends. The most common today is to shrug and say, "That's the way it is." But the scientist who draws his moral premises from spiritual sources does not shrug and does not accept the way things are as being necessarily the way things ought to be.

As a Christian, I see trends in society that I don't like, can't accept, and must work against. But I cannot expect secular society to share my concerns point for point, nor can I impose my views over the will of those involved. I must do more than make the best of the way things are; I must take a particular responsibility for my own family and share responsibilities uniquely for the families of the church of our Lord. We are salt in the general society, but we are *members* of one another in the Christian community, the body of Christ. As Christians, we have decisions to make, ideas to reject, concepts to embrace, and on some issues we need to *fight*. (If we accept the instruction and the disciplines of the Word, we won't often be fighting *against* one another. My view of trends includes the observation that as we encounter more pressure from secular society we have less time and less inclination to waste our resources fighting among ourselves. Hallelujah!)

The key institutions of society are ordained by God in the

Scriptures: church (Matt. 16:18), family (Eph. 5, 6), and civil government (Rom. 13), but that doesn't mean that every family is godly, that every government is Christian, or even that every religious organization is approved by God. Indeed, institutions of all sorts arise from the needs of human society. To say that some institutions are secular and some are sacred is a serious misunderstanding. From a Christian point of view, only the particular religion in which Jesus Christ is glorified and worshiped as Lord might be called a totally nonsecular social institution, and even *it* is shot through with secular influences that make it look like Jesus' description of the great mustard tree loaded down with birds (Mark 4:32). The Christian's family is part of the larger social institution—family. The distinction of the Christian is not in having a family or in believing in one's family but in honoring Christ by establishing or being part of a particular kind of family. If we could get that straight, we would need to worry far less about secular influences.

I am more concerned about erosion than about frontal attacks anyway. For centuries Christians have handled the head-on attacks of evil in society. But the subtle undercutting and washing away in bits and pieces seems to me more dangerous. For example, the self-centeredness that is in the nature of man can be enticed by worldly things even in a Christian family. In a secular society that is materialistic and that measures one's worth by one's properties, the Christian can be gently teased into forgetting Jesus' teaching: "Lay not up for yourselves treasures upon earth" (Matt. 6:19). A question mark must be placed over the ways we stimulate our children to succeed, even over the ways we lay up treasures to provide for them a "good education" and a "good start in life." In reference to the subtle influence of television, I fear the "quiz" and "give-away" shows. Their emphasis on the supposed beauty of gaining goods of financial value seems threatening to the Christian family.

Another specific matter of great concern to me is the subtle undercutting of the marriage relationship. As if the constant bombardment by lewd and vicious views of sex were not enough, a greater threat comes in the form of situation comedies and variety shows that emphasize infidelity and intellectual competitiveness in marriage. As far as I have seen, "Sonny and Cher" is the most damaging show on the air. And frankly, I'm not comfortable with "All in the Family" although surely Archie Bunker's wife, Edith, demonstrates the long-suffering and somewhat dull patience that many in America associate with Christianity. Learning to laugh at human frailties and flaws may be somewhat therapeutic, but the larger effect is to condition us to accept as normal the bickering, competitive, and spiteful behavior that leads to broken marriages.

On another important issue, I am in harmony with those who seek justice, including fair play and equal opportunity. Thus I join in seeking liberation from secular social customs that place men in special authority and power over women in an unbiblical way. But I caution my fellow-liberators that to grasp for women the whole competitive dog-eat-dog system of the "man's world" will be a hollow victory. Far better it would be if we could work from a Christian perspective to reduce the ailment in the secular society's view of the male gender roles that results in a man's *need* to dominate.

The main threat of the public schools is the pressure they put upon our children—pressure to conform, to compete, and to succeed. When the "Christian school" is compared to the public school, it is often hard to spot any major differences. The problem is deeper than whether or not the teacher is a Christian and what sort of sign is over the door; schooling itself, in the pervasive Greek model that is characteristic of Western society, is inherently competitive and success oriented. But, you may ask, isn't this what we need to prepare our children for the realities of society? Wait, just whose realities are we interested in? The Christian is to be a member of a family and of a community, to see individuality, not in terms of "betterness," but in terms of gifts that the Spirit gives one for the benefit of others in the church. This calls for development as a cooperative, serving, and giving sort of person. ("For the love of Christ controls us" [2 Cor. 5:14].) It is inherently non-Christian to enhance the human traits of selfishness, competitiveness, and pragmatic valuing. On this last point, one of the flaws of schooling that even the secular educators are now fretting about is the relativism and pragmatism that leads a person to go to any and all lengths in order to succeed. Pragmatism is shot throughout the whole society, but it focuses its effects on the family through schooling, from nursery school through graduate school.

It is difficult to talk about the influence of secular institutions without becoming overwhelmed in detail. One assumes either that the institutions of secular society each represent a unique influence or that they each contribute some parts to a much larger whole of secular influence. I hold the latter position. That is, I cannot say that certain institutions should bear unique responsibility and guilt.

The school is not a unique influence nor does it pose a unique threat; the "business world" has no distinctly separate moral impact; certainly the service institutions such as hospitals and credit unions carry no moral messages that are apart from the rest of secular influences. Indeed, the only honest way to proceed is to examine the major influences that cut across all the social institutions. In order to decide which are the major influences, we must project them against a backdrop of Christian values and biblical teachings.

In the process of becoming whatever it is that God is making of my life as a disciple and as a scholar, I am gaining certain sensitivities. These sensitivities are like the antennae of the beasts who screen the air about them for alien and dissonant fragments. I have learned to spot pragmatic decision making, especially within the church, wherein we decide what is "right" by asking what works. I have also learned to see the leadership issue Jesus warned about in Matthew 20 and Matthew 23 as he saw the danger of the Greek concept of leadership, that is, leadership as authority and as status. He warned against its corrupting the church even as it had already infected the synagogues at that time. And today it is so thoroughly imbedded in the church we don't even call it a secular influence! I have become sensitive to injustice—especially those that spring from privilege, power, class, sex, race, and position.

Perhaps the most useful way to deal comprehensively with this complex topic is to share what my sensitivities have led me to see as the major whole influences of secular society. These are of particular concern to the Christian family. I refer to these in-fluences as *whole* because they are spread throughout the secular society. They are not the peculiar property or responsibility of any one institution.

Materialism. We live in one of the most materialistic societies in the history of the world. Unhappiness, even to the extremes of suicide and divorce, is the result of placing hope, confidence, and pride in a materialistic and mechanistic society. Some Americans are becoming aware of the horrible ecological effects of over-consumption, extravagance, and waste. The secular society's eco-nomic foundation rests on consumerism, and its children must be taught to buy, buy, buy, eat, eat, eat, and go, go, go or the whole society will fall apart. Materialism causes us to value *things* more than *people.* I see its effects in my own life-style; I complain whenever my children disturb, damage, or deface my "things."

The twin evils of materialism are *competitive greed* and *self-centered individualism.* How deeply these cut into our realization of true community within the body of Christ!

What can we do about materialism within the Christian family? Here are several suggestions:

—Encourage cooperative experiences.
—Set nonmaterialistic goals together as a family; decide to-gether what is worth living for and worth working toward.
—Encourage and affirm one another as being worthy. Remem-ber God gave his Son for each of us.

Faulty communication. Even within the church, much com-munication is one way, simply "telling." The faulty communica-tion styles of the secular institutions, in general, are tending to dehumanize us. Even in our families we see the effects; some-times they are called "communication gaps" or "generation gaps," but at the root they are faulty concepts and faulty habits. The current research in values development reveals a close relation-ship between communication styles within the child's experi-ences and the development of higher structures of values. People were meant to transact, to reason together, and to converse. Look again at Genesis: God began his relationship with the beloved creatures who shared his own image by walking and talking in the garden. From current research we understand that for all of us moral development depends on a freedom to communicate, to share, to seek counsel, to know the accepting fellowship of trustworthy others who are always ready to talk through the dilemmas and the times of disequilibrium.

What can we do to reduce the secular influence of faulty communication?

—Listen to one another with nonjudgmental openness.

—Encourage the seeing of one another's point of view.

—Develop warm and lively communication styles while the going is good. Then the communication lines will be available and open when the rough moments occur.

Relativism. The reason so many church people contend that the public schools should stay out of the area of values education is that the schools have nothing philosophical to offer but the secular society's relativism. The secular society is like a drifting ship with a broken anchor chain. The secular society argues that nothing can be completely trusted, that what works is what counts. Thus pragmatism is rapidly becoming the dominant philosophy, and what is good is what works, and what *is* becomes the norm. How different is the Christian presupposition that what God has said provides a rock-solid basis for knowing what *ought* to be.

Relativism has particularly assaulted marriage. The vows of old are being replaced by fingers-crossed generalizations that are to be respected as long as they work out, until something "better" comes along.

The Christian family can guard itself against relativism in the following ways:

—Help children see marriage in the best possible light.

—Spend time together reading God's Word and discussing its moral meaning.

—Discuss moral and ethical issues and arrive at judgments together.

Deterioration of justice. As the Word of God is pushed farther and farther from the center of human reasoning, injustice becomes more common. The prophets of old were sent time and again with God's invitation to repentance; their voices cried against injustice. Scholars of the Old Testament point out that *righteousness* cannot be defined apart from *justice*. Today's institutions are so thoroughly shot through with injustice that we wonder at God's patience with our society. Let us lift our voices, as of old, crying out against injustice wherever it is seen. We live in a society where might makes right, where authority is equivalent to righteousness. Our families are threatened; somehow we must see to it that God's nature, his justice, love, and mercy become central characteristics of our life-styles and family relationships.

Suggestions for the Christian family:
—Take no privileges based on age, sex, race, prestige, power, or authority.
—Treat one another, even the youngest one, with respect for the dignity of the person.
—Seek relief and resolution of unjust conditions *for all people*.

Some of us tend to see the words *society* and *secular* as interchangeable. The words *secular* and *Christian* or *secular* and *godly* are contrasting terms; *society* can refer to either. Within society there are secular influences and there are Christian or godly influences. But *secular* is not an alternative word for "evil." In fact, many secular institutions have some good within them, even from a Christian's viewpoint. I offer for your consideration Paul's contention in Romans (1:18–20; 2:14, 15) that even those who have never heard (who in one sense are totally secular) have within them a witness of the goodness of God. Thus it is not surprising that even within secular institutions, schooling, for example, certain good intentions and some good outcomes can be seen. If we assume that everything in society is pitched against us and that the influence of God is absolutely limited to the redeemed and to their particular forms of institutions, we mislead ourselves seriously. Isolationism and non-evangelical, introverted stagnation are the sure outcomes of such a theology. The history of the church shows recurrences of asceticism of a most pathetic sort resulting from a loss of kingdom vision. *This is our Father's world.* We are salt within it. Let us continue to lay claim upon the whole world in his name. To do less is to become salt having lost its savor.

9.

Drugs, Adolescence, and the Family

Basil Jackson

At this particular point in human history, the nuclear family is undergoing a more devastating and severe attack than ever before. It is in great danger of disintegrating from both internal and external forces.

Radio, television, and much of what passes for current popular music is part and parcel of family life today. From the psychological point of view, these productions of the media fulfill exactly the same functions as relatively strong tranquilizers. Tranquilizers are medical compounds which affect certain areas of the brain and blot out pain, anxiety, and the pressure of having to think. This is very similar to the effect of much that appears currently in the world of music and entertainment. The nuclear family, as a cohesive unit, does not appear instantly but requires "overcoming." The production of a stable family unit requires the expenditure of energy—it requires work. Such work is most usually the result of the perceived presence of anxiety, and it is a method used to overcome that anxiety. Without such work, family and personal cohesion is gradually eroded.

Much of what appears as advertising in the news media today

Basil Jackson, M.D., is presently chairman of the Department of Psychiatry, Lutheran Hospital of Milwaukee, Milwaukee, Wisconsin, and associate professor to the Department of Psychiatry, Medical College of Wisconsin, Milwaukee, Wisconsin. In addition he has served as visiting professor at Trinity Evangelical Divinity School in Deerfield, Illinois.

also has a similar disintegrating effect on the nuclear family. By far, the majority of television advertising is geared to the pleasure principle rather than the reality principle. People are being conditioned and educated to expect instant solutions for all problems. The pleasure principle is a method of attaining a goal without having to deal with the intermittent steps which may be painful and even anxiety-producing.

The plethora of drugs which has appeared in our society within the last decade is another manifestation of this same disintegrative force. Drugs are not new in our society, but drugs—both legal and illegal, street or prescribed—tend to remove the anxiety which so often is the prerequisite for the work required to produce the cohesion without which no nuclear family can exist.

The fact that we have more and more older people in our society has become an additional problem for the struggling family. At the present time, because of the increased ability of medical care to help the aging survive, the average nuclear family must anticipate taking care of and including more and more people for an increasing period of time. This becomes all the more difficult and disintegrating in terms of the nuclear family because as the family grows so does the proportion of nonproductive people within it.

Automation is another specter in our society which not only depersonalizes the family but depersonalizes the individual. Today, we have become, not just members of a family, but digits and numbers. Our essential personhood and existential value as individuals are becoming less and less important. As the individual becomes less important, so will the family because individuals can only exist within the matrix of interpersonal relationships such as that provided by the family.

Another example of this external disintegrating force is the effect of spectator sports. Today, the plethora of spectator sports leaves us inarticulate and inactive and, in a sense, reduces us to automata. The day of active participation, both physical and psychological, within the realm of family contacts seems to be decreasing, and, for this, a price will be paid.

Numerous external forces are at work in our society which are detrimental and which either overtly or covertly seek to destroy the nuclear family. For example, the very relevance of the family and its usefulness at our particular stage of development of civilization is often questioned. This has been a long and overtly stated goal of Marxism. Psychiatrists and psychologists, unfortunately, also carry much of the blame for this disintegrating force on the family. As the result of new-fangled theories, which often had political bases rather than foundations built on objective data, we have produced a society of ultrapermissiveness and methods of childrearing that not only are antiscriptural but are not supported by proven facts from the behavioral sciences. Within the past decade, the "in" method of childrearing has been to "let the child do its own thing" and to practice permissiveness so as not to "stunt" the innate creativity of the child. Children brought up according to these principles are another example of the biblical admonition regarding the danger of permitting every individual to "do that which is right in his own eyes." Such living according to the immediacy of the moment is, of course, an example of pure pleasure-principle activity. Children raised according to this principle will eventually reject both their families and their parents, according to the same principle, because no one can continue to supply the ever-growing needs and wants which must be satisfied instantly.

The so-called sexual revolution is another example of the increasing practice of the pleasure principle which results in serious negative effects on the nuclear family. When parents live according to a different set of values than those that are God-given, and sometimes than those to which they expect their children to adhere, then automatically their children grow up incorporating the negative values of the double standard. They will suffer from an identity confusion in adolescence related to these double standards foisted upon them by parental authorities.

As the result of disintegrating forces such as those just described, David Cooper, in his vitriolic attack on the family in *The Death of the Family*, says that the bourgeois nuclear family unit, rather than being the matrix for interpersonal contact and communication, has become the ultimate place of nonmeeting. This is, of course, the exact opposite of the divine institution and God's plan.

THE FAMILY AND THE FAÇADE

The family and the home can often be the greatest showpiece on earth in a negative sense. In the home situation, innumerable psychological traumata are committed against the supposed-to-be loved ones. Thus, it is no surprise that, today, in some places, there are almost as many divorces as marriages. In many families who stay together (for whatever reason—economic, social, ego-saving, or theologic), dissension, jealousy, suspicion, hatred, and sexual incompatibility are often the order of the day. Only God knows how many homes are, in reality, houses and not integrated families, and how often the only reason for not seeking divorce is reluctance to obtain such a decree "for the sake of the children," economic support, or avoidance of scandal. When a home is a convenience rather than a family, all types of problems will almost certainly eventually appear, and most of these will be related to poorly developed value systems.

THE BIBLICAL BASIS FOR THE FAMILY

The biblical basis for the family is found in the opening chapters of Genesis as exemplified in the interpersonal relationships which existed among Adam, Eve, and their offspring. This divine institution was not formulated as a result of sin, but, as ordained by God, it preceded the entrance of sin into the world. "And God said, Let us make man in our image, after our likeness; and let them have dominion over the fish of the sea, and over the fowl of the air, and over the cattle, and over all the earth, and over every creeping thing that creepeth upon the earth. So God created man in his own image, in the image of God created he him; male and female created he them. And God blessed them, and God said unto them, Be fruitful, and multiply, and replenish the earth" (Gen. 1: 26–28). "And the Lord God said, It is not good that the man should be alone; I will make him an help meet for him. . . . And Adam said, This is now bone of my bones, and flesh of my flesh" (Gen. 2:18, 23).

No man can live or develop spiritually or psychologically in an interpersonal vacuum. Man has been made a relational creature, and the family has been designed as the matrix within which these relationships—whether horizontal or vertical—may develop and mature.

In Pauline theology, we are again impressed with God's perception of the nuclear family and of its importance because it is used as a model to describe the relationship between Christ and his church. "Wives, submit yourselves unto your own husbands, . . . let the wives be to their own husbands in every thing. Husbands, love your wives, even as Christ also loved the church, and gave himself for it; . . . So ought men to love their wives as their own bodies. He that loveth his wife loveth himself" (Eph. 5:22–28).

Here, the relational aspect of marriage and the family is clearly demonstrated, and Paul is careful to remind us of the continued need for this type of exhortation as the last days approach. "That they may teach the young women to be sober, to love their husbands, to love their children, To be discreet, chaste, keepers at home, good, obedient to their own husbands" (Titus 2:4–5).

Pauline eschatology is very much concerned with the disintegration of the family unit to the point that it would appear reasonable to view such disintegration as one of the predicted signs of the approaching second advent of Christ. "In the last days perilous times shall come. For men shall be lovers of their own selves, . . . disobedient to parents, . . . Without natural affection" (2 Tim. 3:1–3). It would be difficult to improve on this description of the breakdown in the relational functions of the nuclear family as we see them today.

PSYCHOLOGICAL FUNCTIONS OF THE FAMILY

Intimately associated with the relational functions of the nuclear family is the fact that the family serves as the seedbed for conscience and the values which continue to influence thinking, behavior, goals, and morality for as long as a particular individual lives. In spite of its obvious importance, there has been a significant reluctance by behavioral scientists to examine the formation of value systems. The philosopher likes to think of a man's sense of values as being a question of emotion versus reason. The psychologist directs his or her attention to the relationship between the developing value system and the particular instinct characteristics of the human species. The historian elaborates the theme of the growth of conscience in Western civilization while the anthropologist, as the expert in family structure and functioning, traces its emergence from the group morality of the primitive tribe.

On the whole, modern psychology, especially the academic in contrast to the clinical variety, appears quite reluctant to use the term *value system* or to discuss the concept. An examination of the leading works on psychology of the past century reveals that many more psychologists have failed to use the word *conscience* than have used it.

The more modern psychological thinkers, particularly those of the psychoanalytic school, consider personality to have structural divisions or segments which perform separate and specific functions. These parts are not to be considered as concrete realities or self-acting entities but as groups of forces and functions which are dynamically interrelated. The particular area of personality— namely, the conscience—examined in this study is that proposed by Freud who postulated three separate segments within the human personality. However, many of the terms—namely, *id*, *ego*, and *superego*—used to describe these dynamic interrelationships refer to highly metaphorical concepts and only the latter— namely, the superego—will occupy our attention for the present purpose.

The superego is the inhibiting, conscience-including, and repository-of-values component of the personality. It functions to sustain the internalized moral and social values learned from the parents' behavior. It is a conceptualized adviser, admonisher, and threatener, with both conscious and unconscious aspects.

The basic process of organization of this particular function of the personality is advanced by the age of five, but it continues to develop through adolescence and probably through the early adult years. During the period of development, figures of authority capable of punishing or rewarding become incorporated into the personality to form a distinguishable repository of family values.

The superego is derived within the family matrix, primarily

from identification with parents and their substitutes, and herein lies one of the most important psychological functions of the family. Prohibitions and obligations are internalized and incorporated into the unconscious psychological structure of the child. Later, the injunctions and prohibitions of other authorities and of cultural influences are also absorbed into the superego. Still later, the aesthetic and moral demands of one's social group become incorporated, and if stable values have not been internalized earlier from within one's family, trouble becomes inevitable. The superego, as the repository of the value system, may threaten and punish and thereby seek to maintain its authority. It does this by creating anxiety and by producing guilt and remorse. If the superego and the internalized value system which it contains are severe and inflexible, the resulting fear will lead to a rigid, inhibited, anxious, and often neurotic personality.

VALUES AND THE ADOLESCENT IN THE FAMILY

All psychologists agree that adolescence is one of the most difficult periods in life in terms of coping with changes, developing personal identities, and stepping out from the family fold to put to the test the values which have been learned, and hopefully internalized, within the family. All adolescents have two major tasks to accomplish as a prerequisite to further development, and how these tasks are accomplished will, in a large measure, be related to the value systems they have acquired within the nuclear family unit.

The first major task of adolescence is to separate from the family and parents, a prerequisite to being one's own person and to developing a personal identity. Retention of the old family and personal ties becomes more and more uncomfortable as adolescence progresses, and a process of separation must be initiated. Normally, this process takes place gradually, but if the parent, for example, overreacts and does not permit the separation, a relatively abrupt and violent reaction may occur which has the secondary effect of leaving the youngster with an intense, passionate desire for substitute relationships. This explains the "deep and eternal love of today in which tomorrow is forgotten" syndrome. If the separation has not been easy, the new relationships will tend to be characterized by everything which would tend to be distasteful to the original parents and their values. Love may suddenly appear to be transmuted into hate, dependence into open rebellion, respect into contempt and derision. Drugs and other currently available antiestablishment practices suddenly become doubly attractive.

Another characteristic method of hastening the separation process is to become increasingly preoccupied with self. The adolescent suddenly develops inflated ideas of his or her own strength and beauty. At this stage the comb and the mirror are never far away. Unfortunately, with the inflated sense of one's personal strength and ability, aggravated by peer pressures, there often comes the idea of "I can handle drugs; I will be the exception." If value systems developed within the family have not demonstrated that some things are more important than peer-group acceptance and popularity, then resort to drugs may be accepted as the price of initiation. Preoccupation with the body is also often manifested by phobias over acne, blemishes, body odors, and various other body sensations which can be tranquilized by a wide variety of street drugs.

Another method of dealing with the pain and reluctance of separating from the parental figure is to regress psychologically to an earlier stage of development. In effect, the adolescent becomes preadolescent in his psychological functioning. He tends to become more dependent on his parents, and in many cases, unconsciously, parents encourage this type of regression. There will be a tendency to use an excessive amount of identification as a means of molding their own personality to that of the parents as a means of staying with parents rather than separating from them. Adolescents using these particular techniques constantly seem to be asking who they are, where they are, and what they are going to do because, in effect, they are making no progress in stabilizing a separate identity of their own. Their goals tend to be fluid, and they shift from one pseudoidentity to another. When more severe regression occurs, overt psychiatric problems almost always appear. There is disturbance in reality testing, and the individual may end up in a state of confusion to such a degree that he is unable to distinguish between himself and the external world. Again, in my practice, one of the tragedies of this particular problem is that so often, to ease his internal pain and confusion, the adolescent reaches for a variety of street drugs as a method of self-therapy, and these only aggravate the situation.

The second problem the adolescent has to face in his development is coming to grips with his own physical and psychological maturation. In particular, he has to deal with an increasing sense of himself as a sexual object and as having sexual abilities. A common method of dealing with this is to apply excessive repression so that sexual ideas, thoughts, and fantasies are rarely, if ever, permitted on the conscious level. The result is an inhibited, shy, introverted adolescent who, as a means of protecting himself from his own sexuality, will tend to become overly dependent upon his parents, like a child. Again, drugs offer a special attraction to this kind of individual. The psychological effect of most drugs is to act as a social lubricant, and, in effect, they ease the discomfort and pain that many adolescents experience in the peer group situation.

Occasionally, this repression becomes so great that the adolescent develops, not just a dislike for the basic sexual impulses which he is beginning to experience, but a definite antagonism toward them. At this point, he tends to practice the religious asceticism that, at times, resembles elements of Gnosticism. Very often there will be a mistrust of any kind of enjoyment in general, and anything that might even remotely savor of satisfaction of a sexual nature must be completely and absolutely renounced. This manifests a blind fear of all instinctual activities, but the extreme ascetic behavior often manifests sudden swings so that one day the adolescent practices extreme asceticism while the next day he attempts a process of psychological restitution and becomes completely hedonistic. At this stage, he often will be preoccupied with mystical religions, Eastern religions. This kind of preoccupation on an abstract level increases his inability to look at what is going on within him. However, when the sudden vacillation occurs the next day, he may be just as attracted to the pleasures of dope as a means of regaining some of these psychological effects.

SUBSTITUTES, VALUES, AND THE ADOLESCENT

People resort to drugs for a number of reasons, and it is not surprising that the greatest attraction of these agents is to young people in the midst of adolescence with all its turmoil. It would be wrong to say that there is one single answer to the question of why adolescents are attracted to drugs, but some reasons stand out more than others. Basically, the abuse of any kind of drug, whether it is legal or illegal, is an admission of failure to cope with one's internal anxiety and with the world as it is. Some of the commonest reasons for drug abuse that I have seen in my clinical practice with adolescents are as follows.

Experimentation. Many young people experiment with drugs as a response to peer pressure. Fortunately, many of them never repeat the process. Those who become chronic users of a drug tend to have more than the usual degree of adolescent problems, and they seem to be desperately trying to establish some form of psychological homeostasis.

Identification. The process of identification may be one of two sorts. It may be an identification with peers and with the peer group as a means of separating from the parents, or it may be a negative identification in which the adolescent becomes as unlike the parents and their values as possible. If the family beliefs and the family value systems have been very much against drugs, the adolescent may choose drugs as a means of demonstrating individuality, difference, and his or her own identification. Similarly, it may not be so much an antiparental maneuver as part of an initiation fee one pays to be fully accepted in the peer group.

Alleviation from anxiety of any cause. Adolescence is one of the most anxiety-ridden periods in life, and a very common reason for taking drugs at this stage is to treat the anxiety by self-medication. Since anxiety is the outstanding characteristic of this age, it should not surprise us that adolescents are especially afflicted with this malady. Nor should it surprise us that the adolescent should use a variety of pills or alcohol to treat this anxiety when, in effect, although perhaps legally, his or her parents may be doing exactly the same thing.

Mystical preoccupation. It would be very wrong to imagine that the present generation of young people has turned away completely from inner spiritual experience. I believe that, indeed, just the opposite is the case and that adolescents today appear to be searching for authentic religious experience more than at any other time in history. In adolescence the religious and spiritual needs of a person are perhaps more acutely felt because one has not yet gained the calloused quality that so often goes with maturity in the world today. A common story in the American family today is that as our standards of living have gone up our standards of loving have gone down, and no adequate value system will be formulated outside of a milieu of love in the family. When parents try to supply the needs of the growing adolescent with dollars rather than love and compassion, that value will very rapidly be found to be self-destructive.

Spiritual vacuum. By far the most important cause of drug abuse seen in my clinical practice is the existence of a spiritual, religious, and existential vacuum. It seems that young people today, lacking foundational value systems from stable family units, are constantly looking for meaningful models of identification in other places in society. When they fail to find them, they are left to struggle on their own with an increasing sense of frustration, lack of purpose, and meaninglessness. As materialism has become a god, there has been a simultaneous humanization of God. Experience has shown that when such an "adamification" of God occurs there always is a corresponding deification of man. Such a human production of God, however, will always fail to fill a sense of emptiness and to infuse any sense of value, hope, or meaning in the existence of the young person. Thus, again, adolescents become likely prospects for the psychochemical experience, fascination with the occult, and have all the prerequisites for the development of antiestablishment delinquent activities.

RECONSTRUCTION OF THE VALUE SYSTEM

Value systems in our society today are at a low ebb, and this is a direct reflection of the disintegration which has occurred within the family unit. A vacuum exists, not only in the family, but in the adolescent and, indeed, in man everywhere. If this vacuum is not filled by one means, then it will be filled by another. Herein lies the tragedy of the church of the twentieth century. The church possesses a message in the person of Jesus Christ which can give meaning, purpose, hope, and raison d'être and, in the process of making new creatures, will incorporate within man the person of Jesus Christ and all the values he represents.

This is the message of regeneration which we have at our fingertips, and this is the message that we can communicate, not only to individuals, but to families. We can be assured that if we give our all to carrying out this commission not only adolescents but the family, as a unit, will gain new vitality and increased impetus in providing those models of identification and values which are the prerequisite to both individual and national survival.

10.

The Family and Mental Illness

C. Markham Berry

In my boyhood, households commonly included a family member who was disabled. A back room might be reserved for him; his needs were included in the family routine. Today, such a person in the home is unusual and would probably be considered an extraordinary burden for the family. This problem is rarely considered in our meetings on the family. A recent marathon conference concerned with conflicts and tensions in the family lasted some thirty hours but never mentioned this as a home challenge.

Yet pressures are beginning to build up for the family to take into or keep in the home the chronically ill. The increasing age of the population swells the number of old people, many of whom find no happy place to go.[1] The remarkable success of medicine in caring for the acutely ill has shifted medical problems toward those which involve long or permanent disability. For these, our acute-care hospitals have little to offer, and the long-stay, chronic-care facilities are closing.

The most dramatic of these pressures comes from the movement of the mental health care system toward sending the chronic psychotic patient home.[2] In my own state, for example, in the

C. *Markham Berry, M.D.*, is a resident in psychiatry at the Emory University School of Medicine, Atlanta, Georgia, and also serves as senior assistant resident at the Georgia Mental Health Institute. He is the author of numerous articles in the field of psychology and Christianity.

last ten years, over 60 percent of the insane who had been cared for in the back wards of the state mental hospitals have been returned to the community at large.

This movement is also encouraged by a changing social philosophy. The American spirit has traditionally been pragmatic, task oriented, "get the job done." Now it is being replaced by a person-centered view which is more concerned with the needs of people than with their usefulness. It is hard to deny that from this stance, home is a good place for many sick people to be. Joining this plea for home care has been a large chorus of professionals in specialties as diverse as leprosy or maintenance on artificial kidneys.[3] But taking patients into a contemporary home is not as simple as some of these professionals would like us to believe.

The skyrocketing costs of giving considerate, sensitive care in a chronic hospital also bear on the home. To hire an untrained afternoon sitter today costs more than the patient's entire care twenty-five years ago. To provide the necessary additional space in a contemporary home could well cost more than the entire house did then.

While costs have been going up and our philosophy has been becoming more person oriented, our actual life-styles have become activity oriented, more and more favoring the able, the active, and the young. The whole society, including the church, is exerting a centrifugal force on the family. Both children and adults find their meaning, challenges, and even their pleasures outside the home. The home which has become a pit-stop in life makes a poor hospice.

Many families today are struggling to help their children survive the teen years. A teenager or two who have fallen into the morass of drugs, illicit sex, and hedonism can absorb the entire energy reserve and skills of the whole family. A home like this is poorly equipped to take in more trouble.

The chronic patient himself can have a personality which will make home care unthinkable. All of us can remember a home which has been destroyed by a heroic effort to care for an abusive, violent, or uncontrolled patient. Since the home must ultimately define its mission in terms of its ministry to the immediate family, this would be a tragic move however good its intention.

THE DECISION

The decision to take in the sick, then, is complicated, difficult, and somewhat dangerous. Since every member of the household, the marital relationship itself, and the nurturing influence of the home on the growing family are all affected, for better or worse, by the presence of an ill person, the decision should be a family one.

Just as the new member can be destructive, he or she can also be an incredible blessing to the family.[4] For this reason it is an important spiritual decision as well as social and psychological. The family should first feel some assurance that this is God's specific will for them at this time. It is almost certain that later on his will be sought on many occasions, and this prayer will be bolder and more effective if there is an assurance that it is indeed his will!

For those who have had little or no experience of this sort, it would be helpful to consider some of the issues involved.

Stress. The family is a tightly interwoven community, and its interrelationships tend to become more difficult as they become more complex. The disabled person not only adds another personality but brings an illness which itself adds another factor to the family's interactions.

Stress can be a minor factor, however. We cared for a mentally retarded boy in our home for a year or so. Stanley was loving, simple, and quiet. The mechanical care he required was cheerfully distributed through our large family. He created little distress and taught the growing family a good deal. Shortly before he came, a young lady who was bright but suffered from a hysterical personality disorder moved in for a short stay. She kept the entire home in turmoil. We learned from her too but were relieved when she left. It was only then the family could lick its wounds and restore its equilibrium.

Energy. Additional persons, even when they are able to help, add to the work load of the family. Advance thought should be given as to who will do this additional work. We tend to put most of the work burden of the home on the mother; so she is often already overloaded. Much of the hard drudgery has been eased by mechanical devices, but her additional roles of chauffeur, coach, worker, school, Sunday school, teacher and community volunteer have taken up any slack which might have been created. Additional work should either be distributed among other family members or to people or services hired to help.

Sometimes help can be arranged from outside. The household taking the patient in is usually not the only one with some responsibility for his or her care; other siblings or parents may be involved. It is often wise to arrange beforehand for these others to make regular, specific contributions either in time, services, or money. If this has not been clearly arranged in advance, it often turns out to be very difficult to get these others to help later on!

Heart. Perhaps even more necessary than the physical labor involved in caring for the new family member is the heart-energy which is needed. Mother today seems to be the one responsible for the emotional tone and ministry of the home. If the father finds a soft shoulder away from home, if a child is emotionally undernourished, if the home atmosphere is abrasive, we blame mom. Many times the added stress of one more love-starved person is more than she can handle.[5] This load, like the mechanical work involved, can be shared but generally will not be if it is not discussed.

Risk. In some situations, the care of the ill at home represents real risk. The family who takes in a seriously depressed or psychotic person might have to live through a suicide.[6] An older person might fall and break a bone. The lack of skilled care in a home may shorten the life of a patient in other ways. From the patient's point of view these risks are usually happily taken to avoid being in an institution. But the family and others in the home would be wise to consider this risk and knowingly undertake it as part of the overall responsibility for the patient. Too frequently, when something like this happens to an elderly patient, the other children who showed no interest in sharing in the care will be the first to accuse the family of being irresponsible.

Perspective. To care for the sick, one needs to maintain a delicate balance between being close enough to dispense care with loving, individual consideration and yet distant enough to insist that all be done which is needed for this care to be good. This often involves discipline within the framework which allows as much freedom as possible. One must insist that patients assume appropriate responsibility for themselves and their behavior. Within the home this is hard, and it is not unusual for either party to make the other a scapegoat, or for one to lay an unfair burden of guilt on the other.

Ronald R., age thirty-two, is a current schizophrenic patient who is able to get along out of the hospital most of the time. He lives at home and manages expertly to make his mother feel responsible for his antisocial behavior. She has lost the love of her other children, divorced her husband, and now devotes her whole life to mopping up behind Ronald. The real tragedy is that her submission to his whims and her failure to confront him with reality has been just as destructive to him as to all the others.

This happens many times when elderly, senile patients come home. They are often childish, and it is usually necessary to reverse the roles of parent and child. For both, especially for the daughter, this is difficult and sometimes impossible. The elderly though, without some structure in their life, will do poorly. When such patients are moved into a nursing home where discipline is enforced, they can dramatically improve.

With many patients, especially children and the insane as well as the elderly, this discipline is so important that the family would be well advised to get some outside counsel to learn what will be required. Even an evaluation by a third party as to whether the family can give this supporting structure might be advisable.

Occasionally though, a certain amount of laxness works out very well.[7] I always think of Mary S. when this comes up. I knew her in general practice as an elderly, senile patient who stayed with an alcoholic daughter. They lived together easily and mutually supported each other without being abrasive. Once, however, it all got out of hand. The daughter was too drunk, and the mother became confused after a bout of the flu. The household became so disorganized that they both nearly starved. When we discovered what was happening, we put the mother into a nursing home and the daughter into a mental hospital. Within a week or two they were both crying to get back together. None of us were convinced that this would be wise until we saw what had happened to the mother in the nursing home. Sitting around with other deteriorating oldsters, she went downhill so rapidly she was almost unrecognizable. When they moved back into their apartment, they both picked up. The last I heard, a year later, they were much happier and both doing as well as could be expected.

THE CARING

Recognizing then that the decision is somewhat involved, let's assume that the family decides to take the sick patient in or keep the ill family member at home. Some suggestions might be helpful in order to do the job well.

Learn the job. If one felt called to be a teacher, a preacher, or a counselor, he or she would ordinarily plan to get some schooling to fulfill this call. Often some training is also needed to do a good job of nurturing the chronically ill in the home. Each disease has its own personality, its characteristic course, and its challenges. Most diseases produce unique psychological problems in the patient. If someone in the family has set aside some time to prepare for the job, it will be a great help.[8]

Early this year, the police brought in a silent, disheveled young man whom they found standing immobile in the center of an interstate highway. When he came around enough to let us know who he was so we could call his mother, we learned that she was on a farm in Connecticut. She told us briefly and professionally a good deal about her son. She described the medicines which seemed to work well with him and made very practical suggestions as to how we could get him back home when he was able to travel. She turned out to be a widow who had two schizophrenic sons. Her other son did not roam like this one but did well in a simple, rural setting. When her husband died, she sold her home in a wealthy, sophisticated New York City suburb and bought the farm where she cared for her two "patients." No one could have had better care than these boys were getting from their devoted mother. She had come to know a good deal about the disease and more than any physician about her two cases.

Remember the impact on the family. With the considerations mentioned, an ill person within the home can be a constructive influence as well as a benevolent ministry. The large majority of the times I've seen families do this, and when we have done it ourselves, this has been the case. It's necessary though to make certain that the family—especially the children—are indeed thriving and that problems are not growing unawares. Children can easily develop bizarre ideas concerning disease. It is not unusual for children to come to the conclusion that they are in some way responsible for the disability of a person within the home.

A friend described a recent conversation with her brother concerning an illness her mother had when they were children. Both thought that the mother had had a "nervous breakdown." In fact, the mother had gone to the hospital for a hysterectomy. The boy was not emotionally involved in the episode, but the girl felt personally responsible for her mother's downfall. She was certain her noisy boisterousness and argumentativeness had destroyed her mother's mind! When the mother came home from the hospital, the daughter was sent away to relatives for a few weeks, and this confirmed in her mind her personal guilt. Years later, she was still affected by this tragic misunderstanding.

Another friend, undergoing prolonged psychotherapy, feels much of her present difficulty stems from the fact that her mother never kissed her, rarely allowed her to come close, and carefully avoided caressing her. Years later, she discovered that the mother had once cared for a tubercular uncle and was dreadfully afraid she was still contaminated. Her coldness actually was an effort to avoid giving the daughter TB. But the daughter thought, until she was an adult, that there was something horribly bad about her that made her mother avoid her!

Since this sort of thing is possible, it's a good idea to keep open lines of communication within the family concerning the impact of the person and his or her illness. School-aged children should be quizzed occasionally to assure that they understand what is going on.[9]

THE PSYCHOTIC PATIENT

The old, large, state mental hospitals which were designed to remove the insane from sight and memory are becoming relics of the past. It has been proven again and again that these patients are much happier and better cared for at home or at least in the community at large.[10] Families, neighbors, and nearby community mental health centers are bringing a variety of support services to the home patient. Walk-in crisis centers, day hospitals, home nursing visits, call-in consultations, and out-patient individual and group therapy are now widely available.[11] These reduce symptoms and cut down on the repeated psychotic breaks which could require rehospitalization. When problems occur, they are rarely dangerous, and the patient is often quickly and effectively returned home. In the state mental hospital unit where I work, the average stay is less than three weeks!

Even with all these services available, there will still be problems. It might be helpful to outline some of the critical areas these problems involve.

Conflicts. Most emotionally disturbed people are particularly hassle-sensitive.[12] The schizophrenic, for example, has difficulty feeling his way into an interpersonal conflict and reacting appropriately.

Donny D. was admitted to our unit last winter following a break which started with a family argument. His mother, an ex-alcoholic, was also suffering from terminal cancer and had been pleading with Donny to bring beer home to her. His father bitterly resented her reversion to alcohol and took it out on Donny, giving him a tongue-lashing and forbidding him to buy her any more alcohol. This did not quiet the mother though, and Donny was caught between the two. He ran away from home and became so disorganized that he landed in jail. He ultimately was admitted to the state hospital. Now that the family better understands Donny's particular sensitivity, he is doing well at home after some five months.

Communication. Many students of schizophrenia have identified patterns of communication which are common in the homes these patients are raised in.[13] These involve distorted meanings, silences in which important things are left unsaid, dark family secrets never discussed, and double messages in which the words and the emotional tone don't jibe. Any person with a mental problem finds these confusing and wearing. They frequently make him or her lose confidence in his or her ability to communicate with normal people. Patients get along better in a hospital or living alone than dealing with these factors. The family which cares for the psychotic patient must be patient, consistent, and explicit in the way it communicates.[14]

Respect. The mental patient, usually more or less disabled, is often more sensitive to his or her uselessness than even most professionals are aware of.[15] He or she is often willing to take on a job far beneath his or her capacity just to feel useful in the working community.[16] The mental patient should be treated fairly, given neither more nor less favor than peers or siblings. While he or she will have limitations and will need some support, this should be given without condescending or putting too much pressure on him or her to perform tasks that are impossible.[17]

The psychotic patient has traditionally been considered foolish, awesome, and a little demonic. Most of them are none of these.[18] Those willing to understand them find themselves greatly enriched and broadened by their friendships. Through the bizarre distortions one frequently finds in the schizophrenic, one gets a deep look into what being human really means. The peculiar insights and sensitivities of these people must be respected and valued before they share these treasures. It is time well spent for anyone.

A "now" orientation. Psychotic patients are encouraged by being in an environment which emphasizes the "now." Past failures and experiences are best put behind. Aside from an optimistic atmosphere of hopefulness, the future with its grim realities should also be played down. When the patient begins to improve, this sometimes becomes a critical problem. He or she realizes for the first time that he or she will never really have a normal life. Marriage and a family, a responsible challenging place in society, may never be. At the same time the patient might be getting better organized and strong enough to carry out his or her own suicide. Diverting the patient's thoughts to his or her present, improving life can be all-important.

It would be grossly unfair to leave this discussion on such a pessimistic note. There are few fields of service which can be more richly rewarding than caring for the sick, the senile, or the psychotic in the home. I challenge the reader to ask the next person he or she meets who has done this and done it cheerfully and well whether this is not so. A glimpse of this would best come from two people who are quoted below. The first is from a patient.

> Living with schizophrenia can be hell, because it sets one so far apart from the trend of life followed by the majority of persons today but seen from another angle it can be really living, for it seems to thrive on art and education, it seems to lead to a deeper understanding of people and liking for people, and it's an exacting life, like being an explorer in a territory where no one else has ever been. I am often glad that illness caused my mind to "awaken" 11 years ago, but there are other times when I almost wish that it would go back to sleep. For it is a constant threat. A breakdown in physical health, too much pressure, too many responsibilities taken on because they sound interesting to the "well" side of me, and I could be plunged back into the valley. Am I to live in a chair on a basement ward of a mental hospital, forced to endure a meaningless existence because people don't know how important freedom is to survival or am I to move ahead to find a place in the modern world outside hospital walls? It's like being on a swing.[19]

The final word comes from Dr. Otto Allen Will, Jr., a physician who has devoted the bulk of his working life to intensive therapy with schizophrenic patients.

> The therapeutic process is concerned with the development of the relatedness of patient and therapist and a study of the antecedents, the course and the vicissitudes of the development. Relatedness, insight, and action increase together. Therapy is a process of growth marked by mutuality, in which one participant cannot alter without the other. The therapist learns from his patient and grows with him; it could not be otherwise.[20]

NOTES

1. H. B. Brotman, "Every Tenth American: Adding Life to Years," *Bulletin of the Institute of Gerontology*, University of Iowa 15 (1968): 3–7.

2. G. H. Wolkon, "Effecting a Continuum of Care: An Exploitation of the Crisis of Psychiatric Hospital Release," *Community Mental Health Journal* 4 (1968): 63–73.

3. G. H. Wolkon, M. Karmen, and H. T. Tanaka, "Evaluation of

a Social Rehabilitation Program for Recently Released Psychiatric Patients," *Community Mental Health Journal* 7 (1971): 312–22.

4. R. L. DuPont, R. G. Ryder, and H. U. Grunebaum, "An Unexpected Result of Psychosis in Marriage," *American Journal of Psychiatry* 128 (1971): 735–39.

5. M. A. Berezin, "Partial Grief in Family Members and Others Who Care for the Elderly Patient," *Journal of Geriatric Psychiatry* 4 (1970): 53–64.

6. J. A. Chapman, "The Early Symptoms of Schizophrenia," *British Journal of Psychiatry* 112 (1966): 255–61; Alvin I. Goldfarb, "Maladjustments of the Aged," in *American Handbook of Psychiatry*, 2d ed., edited by Silvano Arieti (New York: Basic Books, 1974), 2:833.

7. L. H. Robinson, "Group Work with Parents of Retarded Adolescents," *American Journal of Psychotherapy* 28 (1974): 397–408.

8. Howard E. Freeman and O. G. Simmons, "Consensus and Coalition in the Release of Mental Patients," *Human Organization* 20 (Summer 1961): 89–91.

9. Ozzie G. Simmons, J. A. Davis, and H. Spencer, "Interpersonal Strain in Release from a Mental Hospital," *Social Problems* 4 (1956): 21–28.

10. A. H. Collins, "Natural Delivery Systems: Accessible Sources of Power for Mental Health," *American Journal of Orthopsychiatry* 43 (1973): 46–52; L. R. Mosher, Alma Menn, and S. A. Matthews, "Evaluation of a Home-based Treatment for Schizophrenia," *American Journal of Orthopsychiatry* 45 (1975): 445–67; Benjamin Pasamanick, F. R. Scapitti, and Simon Dinitz, *Schizophrenics in the Community* (New York: Appleton-Century-Crofts, 1967); R. E. Meyer, L. F. Schiff, and A. Becker, "The Home Treatment of Psychotic Patients: An Analysis of 154 Cases," *American Journal of Psychiatry* 123 (1967): 1430–38; John P. Spiegel, "The Family: The Channel of Primary Care," *Hospital and Community Psychiatry* 25 (1974): 785–88; R. J. Swann, "A Survey of a Boarding Home Program for Former Mental Patients," *Hospital and Community Psychiatry* 24 (1973): 485–86.

11. R. L. Pearlman, M. Hecht, S. Blackman, and R. M. Silberstein, "An Acute Treatment Unit in a Psychiatric Emergency Service," *Hospital and Community Psychiatry* 24 (1973): 489–91; E. L. Rabiner, H. Molinsky, and A. Gralnick, "Conjoint Family Therapy in the Outpatient Setting," *American Journal of Psychotherapy* 16 (1963): 618–31; R. S. Rybach, "Schizophrenics Anonymous, a Treatment Adjunct," *Psychiatry in Medicine* 2 (1971): 247–53; Robert J. Greene and Frank G. Muller, "A Crisis Telephone Service in a Nonmetropolitan Area," *Hospital and Community Psychiatry* 24 (1973): 94–97.

12. Geoffrey G. Wallis, "Stress As a Predictor in Schizophrenia," *Annual Review of the Schizophrenic Syndrome 1973*, ed. Robert Chancro (New York: Brunner/Mazel, 1974).

13. E. G. Mishler and N. E. Waxler, "Family Interaction Processes and Schizophrenia, a Review of Current Theories," *Merrill-Palmer Quarterly* 11 1965): 296–316.

14. J. R. Schuerman, "Marital Interaction and Posthospital Adjustment," *Social Casework* 53 (1972): 163–72.

15. R. Moos and J. Schwartz, "Treatment Environment and Treatment Outcome," *Journal of Nervous and Mental Diseases* 154 (1972): 264–75.

16. Howard Freeman and Ozzie Simmons, *The Mental Patient Comes Home* (New York: John Wiley and Sons, 1963).

17. George Howard, "The Ex-mental Patient As an Employee," *American Journal of Orthopsychiatry* 45 (1975): 479–83.

18. S. Page, "The Elusive Character of Psychiatric Stigma," *Canada's Mental Health* 22 (1974): 15–17.

19. Norma MacDonald, "Living with Schizophrenia," *The Inner World of Mental Illness*, ed. Bert Kaplan (New York: Harper and Row, 1964), p. 184.

20. Otto Allen Will, Jr., "Human Relatedness and the Schizophrenic Reaction," *Psychiatry* 22 (1959): 205–23.

The Family Reaching Out

11.

Friendship Evangelism

Matthew S. Prince

Christ left us one great commission, to go into all the world and announce the good news to every person, making disciples as we go (Matt. 28:18–20, Mark 16:15, Acts 1:8, John 20:21). We do not have an assortment of great commissions, only one. Jesus specifically said that we were to begin at Jerusalem, at home. There are only two possible responses—obedience or disobedience. If a believer is involved in the Great Commission, his or her home will be involved. The biblical truths about husband-wife relationships, parent-child relationships, and couple-Christ relationships make it inconceivable that a husband and wife could be involved without the home being included to some degree.

My wife and I met a couple who were experiencing great difficulties with life, marriage, and religion. We began inviting them often to our home. New Life discussions were being held, and they were asked to join. After several months they both trusted Christ. The woman explained that they had searched in various religions and activities for God but had been unable to find him. In the relaxed, loving atmosphere of our home and their home these people had come to understand that Christ is God's

Matthew S. Prince, founder and president of New Life, Inc., was for many years a practicing attorney and a pastor.

son, that he loved us, that he lived the perfect life God requires, and that he died for all our wrongs at the cross, finally conquering death for us. They learned and experienced the beautiful truth of personally receiving him. She summed it up when she said, "All my life I wanted to know the Lord but never knew how. No one ever told me until you." That couple is now actively serving Christ in the church and in the community, and they have led many to him in their home.

That day in Jericho when Christ met Zaccheus, two remarkable things happened. First, he told Zaccheus that he would stay at his house (Luke 19:5), then he revealed the motivation for his incarnation, "For the Son of man is come to seek and to save that which was lost" (Luke 19:10). We serve a seeking Savior. When our hearts quit seeking, we have left his heart. If we love him, then our hearts will beat where his heart beats. The Christian home should be a seeking home. If we are concerned only with our well-being as a family unit and never reach beyond ourselves, then we are not following the heart of Jesus Christ.

A leading pastor said that one trouble in Christianity is that we are trying to build a "cloistered group of institutionally domesticated Christians." Many of us have become familiar with the phenomenon reflected in the phrase "the holy huddle"—Christians who through excessive introspection spend all their time on themselves. Having a balanced, healthy, harmonious Christian home is one of the best things that can be accomplished in life, but it is not the top priority item. The Great Commission is. Being a husband and a father of six I am extremely sensitive to the value of such a home. However, the Christian world faces a real and present danger of total obsession with the good to the exclusion of the best. Suppose we have the most psychologically healthy and practically balanced homes in all the world. It means a lot now in terms of priceless people. What difference will it make a million years from now? If what Jesus Christ says is true, then it will have meaning only if others are in heaven as a result of the witness that home bore here on earth. In all our attention to the Christian home we should emphasize Christ's first priority, going to others that they might become disciples of his.

THE BIBLICAL PATTERN

Christ lived out a great deal of his ministry in homes. He ministered to Peter's mother-in-law and others in Peter's home (Mark 1:29–32). In his home at Capernaum, Jesus taught a house full of people and healed the paralytic who was let down through the roof (Mark 2:1–12). Immediately after his call to be a follower of Christ, Levi gave a reception in his home with Christ as the guest of honor so that his tax-gathering friends and others could meet his Lord (Luke 5:29–32). Christ taught and served in the home of Simon the Pharisee (Luke 7:36–50) and in the home of Mary, Martha, and Lazarus (John 12:1–11) where people had an opportunity to observe and believe in him.

God has emphasized the importance of Peter's ministry in Cornelius's home by preserving that record in two chapters of his Word (Acts 10, 11). Paul carried on an effective ministry for eighteen months in the Corinth home of Titius Justus (Acts 18:7, 11). When he met with the Ephesian elders at Miletus, the apostle reminded them how he taught publicly and "from house to house" (Acts 20:20).

In contemporary religion, we have become so meeting conscious, crowd conscious, and technique conscious that we are in danger of overlooking the strategic value of the home in carrying out the Great Commission. In the biblical pattern of reaching others for Christ, the home plays a significant role.

THE LOGICAL PLACE TO DEMONSTRATE LOVE

In explaining his ministry to the Corinthians, Paul unveiled many of the secrets that made him a power for Christ. In getting to the heart of his ministry he described the driving dynamic that controlled his life. "For the love of Christ controls us" (2 Cor. 5:14, RSV). The verb *controls* is interesting. It refers to basic motivation. Paul did what he did because Christ's love urged him.

Why do we talk to people about Jesus Christ? What should control our relationships with them? All too frequently we are led to believe that those without Christ are the enemy. They are victims of the enemy. Christians sometimes create hostile atmospheres by initial attitudes toward those that are without Christ. The fruitful Christian life should be motivated by love. The believer should decide whether or not he or she genuinely loves that person Christ loves and for whom he died.

In an earlier part of Paul's detailed explanation of his life and ministry, he explains that unbelievers are superhumanly blinded by Satan (2 Cor. 4:3–4). He then gives God's three-part formula for piercing the satanic darkness: first, the focus on Christ (2 Cor. 4:5); second, the believer the bond-slave of the unbeliever for Christ's sake (2 Cor. 4:5); and third, our love for the one without Christ (2 Cor. 4:6). The one who has been satanically blinded can see the face of Jesus Christ through the darkness. Where will he or she see it? In our hearts. That is where God has shone to give the light of the knowledge of his glory in the face of Christ. It is not our intellects or brilliant abilities to argue, but in our hearts.

What more logical place to demonstrate love to a person than in the home? In fact the home may offer more potential for showing the love of Christ than any other vehicle available to us. The last social barriers are torn down when an individual is invited into the home. When Christians meet with non-Christians, the atmosphere should be so lovingly receptive that the unbeliever will go away feeling more welcome than any place he or she has ever been.

Some time ago in New Life a man and his wife attended a discussion series of four weeks, each session meeting in a different home. When asked why they knew the Bible was God's Word or knew that Jesus Christ worked, Christians frequently responded that among other things he changed lives for the better. The man without Christ said he was tired of hearing about changed lives and wanted to hear some other explanations concerning why he should believe in Christ. Although intellectually he objected to hearing about changed lives, he continued to come to the home of Christian friends because of what he experienced there. Beyond the thinking process he became emotionally involved. He could not question the reality of the love which he and his wife experienced. Today he knows Christ as Savior and is helping win others.

When Paul went to Thessalonica, he won many people to Christ. In describing his ministry to them he said that he loved them so much he wanted to give them not only the gospel message but also his life because they were very dear to him (1 Thess. 2:8). That is effective Great Commission business. We are called to make disciples, not converts. The most effective work for Jesus Christ is done, not through simply distributing literature, but in sharing our lives with people.

The Wisdom Walk

In Colossians 4:2–6 Paul discusses how the believer should relate to the person without Christ. In verses 2 through 4 he emphasizes the necessity of devoted, alert prayer for open doors and clarity of the gospel. He then says that we are to conduct ourselves with wisdom toward outsiders, making the most of the opportunity, seasoning our speech with salt suitable to the individual taste of the person to whom we should respond (vv. 5–6). There is nothing spiritual about being foolish, crude, rude, or insensitive to the lives of others. It is biblical to be wise (v. 5) and sensitive (v. 6) with those who do not have Christ.

Consider how wise it is to use the home as a means of touching those who are without. From the standpoint of the home itself, the whole family can be involved. It is a good way to let children and every member of the household see what marvelous things happen when others hear of Jesus Christ. When group sessions or individual contacts are made in the home, each family member is aware of what is going on. God honors a home for this kind of Great Commission activity.

Many are hostile toward religious buildings and religious meetings. The personal threat is so great that they will not even consider getting near such a building. Every human being is reluctant in some measure to attend strange meetings where he or she will be surrounded by strange people.

By contrast, consider what the Christian home offers. An invitation to the home proves that the host cares for the friend without Christ. The atmosphere is casual. Informal conversation at genuine heart level can be carried on without pretense. Relaxation is real. Openness naturally results. When done properly, nothing can be more effective than the wise application of a loving home atmosphere in which people can receive Christ and learn to grow in him.

A very successful businessman and his wife trusted Christ through New Life. He wanted his partner Jim to know Christ. He invited my wife and me to his home, explaining that he was inviting the partner and his wife the same night for dinner hoping that I could lead him to Christ. Now this unbeliever was very defensive to anything about the Lord.

I assured the new Christian that I would come to his home but only on the condition that we would not talk about the Lord. He looked shocked. However, it simply would not have been wise to attempt any kind of "gang up" on the non-Christian. He would be looking for that. We would let him initiate any conversation about the Lord. My friend agreed.

When the night came, things happened exactly as expected. Jim immediately began to needle our hostess. He knew he could make her mad by saying certain things about God. He said, "If there is a God, I don't think he should be mad at me. I've never done anything wrong."

My response was, "That's interesting, do you play the guitar?" He said no, and when asked what he liked to do as a hobby, he explained in depth. This happened several times before dinner.

When we sat down to eat, Jim brought up the subject again, "Seriously, if someone knew a lot about evolution and somebody else knew a lot about the Bible, I'll bet they would have a lot to say to each other."

"I answered, "I'm sure they would, but I don't know anything about that. Would you like some more beans?" He said yes and finished off the beans.

We returned to the living room where he tried to bring up the subject two or three more times. Finally I asked him a personal question with his agreement. "Jim, are you one of those religious fanatics?" He of course said no. Why did I want to know? I responded that he had tried to talk about God all night, and I just thought he might be one of those religious fanatics. Immediately he sensed that we all cared for him and did not want to fight. Within six months he became a Christian. He felt love in his partner's home. All the arguments could not overcome the warm acceptance of a Christian home.

COMMON GROUND

Five times in a few short sentences Paul expressed his determination to win others to Christ (1 Cor. 9:19–22). He was not content with merely sowing the seed; he wanted to see people won to Christ.

This is perfectly scriptural. Christ taught a harvest theology, not just a search theology, as is evidenced in the story of the lost sheep and the lost coin (Luke 15:3–10). He also taught harvest theology in John 4:35–38 and in Matthew 9:37–38. Paul followed Christ's heart.

In his determination to win others the apostle severely disciplined himself (1 Cor. 9:26). He described his method, "Yes, whatever a person is like, I try to find common ground with him so that he will let me tell him about Christ and let Christ save him" (1 Cor. 9:22, LB). How can we best become all things to all men, finding common ground from which we can lead them to Christ? What better vehicle than the home where people can speak what is honestly in the heart?

Five years went by before one friend let me tell him about Christ. He constantly said, "We are friends," and then would tell me confidential things in his heart. He needed someone to talk with. For several years I was his attorney. We worked through some difficult times together. Finally one day in my home while we were alone in the study, he prayed to receive Christ. I believe he would have come to Christ much sooner had I invited him to my home earlier. After we began to visit in the home, after he and his wife became acquainted with my wife, significant progress occurred. It took us a long time to establish the common ground. From that base he was able to move to a personal reception of Christ through the unique bond we felt in the warm glow of the study where true friends met to share confidences.

THE GENTLE CORRECTION

In his last letter to Timothy, Paul has a lot to say about how Christians should lead others to Christ. Three times in chapter 2

(vv. 14, 16, 23) he says that we are not to fight. He then gives specific instructions concerning what we are to do. "And the Lord's bond-servant must not be quarrelsome, but be kind to all, able to teach, patient when wronged, with gentleness correcting those who are in opposition; if perhaps God may grant them repentance leading to the knowledge of the truth, and they may come to their senses *and escape* from the snare of the devil, having been held captive by him to do his will" (2 Tim. 2:24-26, NASB).

In most formal or even informal Christian meetings, either an overt or hidden agenda must be kept. Usually many more people are involved and things are far too impersonal for gentle correcting. I am heartily in support of the Christ-honoring church and always have been and by the grace of God always will be involved in it. Much gentle correcting has taken place, can take place, and will take place in the church. However, the home provides a uniquely fitting place for carrying out this witness.

How much that goes on in the name of witnessing is nothing more than fighting? An invitation to the home immediately eliminates the concept of quarrelsomeness. It reflects an attitude of receptivity and togetherness. Through Christ-honoring conversation, either in small groups or individually, the person can come to his or her senses and perhaps escape from Satan's trap.

Overcoming the Biggest Obstacles

In over a quarter of a century's experience as pastor, missionary and practicing attorney I have come to the conclusion that in all witnessing two steps consistently are more difficult than others. The first is bringing up the subject, and the second is closing the transaction.

The Christian home offers a thousand and one ways for Christ to become the object of discussion. All of these can be natural, unforced introductions to him.

A business leader came to a home session at the invitation of his friends who were our hosts. After several weeks he and I cultivated a satisfactory friendship. In a few months it became an intense friendship. One night standing in the basement of his house he asked why I was so concerned that he have Christ. My answer was simple: "Tom, it's hard for one man to tell another this, but frankly if you are not in heaven when I get there then I do not want to go." He trusted Christ. In that setting only three people were involved. He was at ease in his own home and could respond only to the Lord and to me.

Extraneous interruptions can be eliminated. A receptive atmosphere can be maintained. The two biggest hurdles can be overcome.

A Home Saturated with Joy

Christ taught the same truths two times when he told of the lost sheep and the lost coin (Luke 15:3–10). In both cases there was great sensitivity to the need of the lost one. Each person put forth a concerted effort until the lost was found and brought home. The result of each was individual and corporate joy.

Christ said (John 15:11) that he desired his joy to be in us and for our lives to be saturated with this joy. The word he uses suggests a great sense of well-being. It is Christ's desire that our lives be characterized by great well-being which transcends circumstances. Leading other people to Christ can bring more joy than anything else in Christian experience.

In emphasizing the urgency of the imminent harvest Christ said that gathering fruit for life eternal results in rejoicing (John 4:36). The home that is involved in the Great Commission will experience Christ's kind of fulfilling joy.

In one instance my wife and children were interested in another family. We began to have them in our home, and we went to their home. Within one week the father and mother became certain of their relationship with the Lord, and one of the children through one of my children and some friends did the same. We have had a special relationship with them ever since, and the benefits to our home have been considerable. Nothing can replace the warm glow such experiences produce.

Part of the fruit of the spirit is joy (Gal. 5:22–23). The home that is involved in the Great Commission will reflect Christ's sense of well-being and will be a home where heaven's joy can be found.

12.

The Family—
Foundation for Evangelism

Leighton Ford

Christian groups have mushroomed in amazing fashion in the last twenty-five years. The sportsmen have their Fellowship of Christian Athletes, women their Christian Women's Clubs, and businessmen their CBMC. Students join together in Inter-Varsity, Campus Crusade, Young Life, and Campus Life. Stewardesses and pilots encourage each other in the Fellowship of Christian Airlines Personnel, show people in the Christian Arts Fellowship, and politicians simply through the Fellowship! Pro golfers and their wives have weekly Bible studies on the tour, and the men who drive the transports are in Truckers for Christ!

I praise God for these groups by which salt and light of the gospel are penetrating our vocational and special interests. But how ironic it would be if we default in our evangelism at the most crucial point of all—the family!

How can we evangelize non-Christian families? How can we get Christian families vitally involved in sharing their faith?

This challenge was pointed up for me by two recent conversations. The first was with a young man, part of whose ministry is to run six homes where young people from Christian homes are taken in for nine months at a time. For the most part these are

Leighton Ford is vice-president of the Billy Graham Evangelistic Association. He alternates with Billy Graham on the "Hour of Decision" which is carried over hundreds of radio stations. He is also the author of *New Man, New World*.

youths in their late teens for whom Christianity is unreal, in spite of their believing parents. A major problem, he has found, is that they have been so spiritually isolated that they have seldom seen the power of the gospel really at work. Their families have little contact with the non-Christian "world" and seldom, if ever, share their faith. So he and his staff disciple them, involve them in personal evangelism, and see many of them come spiritually alive for the first time as they say, "Hey, all this I've learned about Jesus is more than words. It really works! He does change lives!"

My second conversation was with a representative of the Navigators who has been working in Brazil. Much of his ministry has been with Marxists, and a lot of it has been through the home. He has found many Marxists quickly grasp the teaching of the gospel on an intellectual level, but they are not moved to consider and respond until they see it fleshed out in relationships. One man accepted Christ after being exposed to the gospel over a two-year period. "It wasn't just what you said," he explained. "The turning point came when you had me to your home for dinner. One of your children misbehaved, and I saw how you disciplined him in love. The reality of God's presence was there, and that's when I decided to turn my life over to Christ."

Two dilemmas face us: how to reach non-Christian families and how to turn on Christian families that have the spiritual blahs. But these are actually two parts of one dilemma! Non-Christian families are often unreached because Christian families have the blahs! But those two conversations so close together made me realize there is *one* solution that affects both problems. Get the "Christian" families to reaching the non-Christian families, and the unreached will be reached and the Christians may get over the blahs.

Biblical Evangelism: A Family Affair

In the Bible, evangelism is very much a family affair. Salvation itself is family-oriented. The living God (and the Trinity is in a very real sense a family!) has made himself known to us as Father. The best definition I know of a Christian is one who through the new birth has God as his Father. Adoption into God's family is the highest blessing of the gospel! By faith we are justified; justification is a *legal* idea and sees God (correctly) as *judge.* But adoption is a *family* idea and sees God as Father! This is especially exciting to me because I myself am an adopted child. I have always been thankful that my parents chose me to be their own; they didn't *have* to, but they did, and God has done the same.

British theologian J. I. Packer points out that being God's adopted children should control our whole life-style. We are to imitate the Father, Jesus said, loving our enemies as our Father in heaven does (Matt. 5:44). We pray to "Our Father in heaven," knowing he is always available (Matt. 6:9). We walk by faith because we believe our Father anticipates our needs and will supply them (Matt. 6:25). Earth is the place where God wants us to bear the family likeness of his Son (Rom. 8:28). And heaven will be a grand family reunion!

Through evangelism we want people everywhere to be able to say, "I am a child of God. God is my Father. Heaven is my home. Jesus is my brother, and so is every Christian!"

The family was a high priority in God's purpose as it unfolded. In the Old Testament the family head would pledge allegiance to the Lord for his household: "As for me and my house, we will serve the Lord" (Josh. 24:15). The Jewish family was a kind of visual aid to demonstrate God's grace. Many Gentiles became proselytes because the spiritual solidarity of the Jewish family made a tremendous impact on them.

Through Jesus, God zeroed in on the family. Scan the Gospel of Luke, and you'll see how true this is. The Savior came to bless the world and was introduced through two faithful families (Luke 1, 2). Jesus and his disciples used homes—Levi's and Martha and Mary's and Zacchaeus's—as headquarters to reach and teach (Luke 5:29, 10:38, 9:12, 10:5, 19:5). A dinner party was often the setting for Jesus' message (Luke 5:29, 7:36, 14:1). He helped families and widows in trouble, healing Peter's mother and Jairus's daughter, bringing back to life the widow of Nain's son (Luke 4:38, 8:41, 7:11). Home life gave him many of his best illustrations—his parables of the friend who comes at midnight (Luke 11:5), the wedding feast (Luke 14:1), the prodigal son (Luke 15:1). Concern for family life comes through clearly in what Jesus teaches about divorce (Luke 16:18) and about blessing children (Luke 18:15) or causing them to stumble (Luke 17:1).

Yet Jesus also makes clear that there is a higher allegiance, that loyalty to the Father takes first place even over family ties! His Father's business was top priority in his own life, though he willingly submitted to his parents (Luke 2:41). His family was made up, not just of his mother and brothers in the flesh, but of all those who do God's will (Luke 8:31). When he called disciples, he spelled out that it might involve a break with their families (Luke 9:58, 14:26). But any sacrifice they might make in leaving home would be repaid; God would give them a hundred homes in his wider family (Luke 18:28)!

A STRATEGY OF FAMILY EVANGELISM

A strategy of family evangelism must have at least three parts: (1) leading members of Christian families to personal faith; (2) evangelizing non-Christian families; (3) developing Christian families as a base for evangelism.

Evangelism in the Christian Family

How can believing spouses and children best lead their non-Christian partners or parents to the Lord? That is a large and important question, but an even more important question is, How are we to evangelize the children of Christian parents so they can be Christ-bearers to their peers?

The problem of the "second generation" has been recognized, and I hope the research results will give us valuable insights. Nominal, hand-me-down Christianity has plagued every age (for example, the great debate over the Half Way Covenant in colonial New England), every church (whether they practice infant or believer's baptism), and every part of the Christian world (see Stephen Neill, The Unfinished Task [London: Lutterworth Press, 1957], pp. 35ff.). And it touches every parent! Many of us have ached when our children seemed indifferent or rebellious to the Lord we love. And many of us have praised God when we saw them begin to show signs of their own precious faith!

Theologian Henri Blocher suggests that the Bible sets forth

three basic positions relevant to the evangelism of our children:
(1) faith is *not hereditary;* (2) there is a *spiritual* solidarity to
the family; (3) the child is not already a responsible person; he
becomes one.

Discipleship involves a personal faith and commitment. As
Corrie Ten Boom says, "God has no grandchildren!" The problem is shared by the Christian home and the Christian church.
It's easy enough to get children or church members to *comply*
with the words we ask them to say or the rituals in which we ask
them to take part. It's also fairly simple to get children or church
members to *identify* with the faith of their parents or some person they admire. But what God desires and what we seek are children and church members who will *internalize* their faith until it's
really theirs. What we want is not just proselytes or semiconverts
but *disciples* who follow Jesus as Lord!

To this cause the "spiritual solidarity of the family" is an ally,
not an enemy. "The promise is unto you, and to your children,"
said Peter (Acts 2:39). As a Christian parent, I can claim God's
promise on behalf of my children, believing, even when the
blossoms or fruit haven't yet appeared, that God intends to call
my children to himself! But this faith is meant to spur me as a
parent to my spiritual responsibility, not to leave it to God or
others.

As a Christian parent, I have to ask myself: Do I realize that in
God's plan my wife and I are to be the first evangelists of our
children, that I have no greater priority? Billy Graham has cau-
tioned my wife and me several times not to try to win the world
and lose our own children. Judge Keith Leenhouts, author of
A Father—A Son—And a Three-Mile Run, tells of the time and
love he spent with his son Bill, a slow learner. Over the years,
affirmed by his father's love, Bill made it into college and over-
came his lack of physical coordination to become an all-state
runner. "To the best of my ability," writes Leenhouts, "I
wrapped up my love for Bill in my heart, body, mind and soul
so that the word *love* truly became flesh. If Bill in and through
my flesh could sense the love of God and give God his love, then
I had done my job as a father. If not, I had failed. To me, it was
that simple."

Do I realize how crucial it is that my wife and I model the gospel in our relationships in the home? Children learn through watching the behavior of their parents. They see love and justice and mercy "dramatized," or they don't. And that's what gives telling force to the words and teaching they hear! "Discipleship," says Juan Carlos Ortiz, "is not a communication of knowledge, but a communication of life." Discipleship is built by life upon life!

A few weeks ago Chip, a senior football player at a prep school, accepted Christ in a meeting where I spoke. "I've been wanting Christ for months!" he said. "It's all because of the change I saw in my parents when they accepted Christ early this year. Before, they couldn't get along. Now they love each other!"

Do I as a parent teach my children in God's ways? As the old saying goes, we need to walk the talk and talk the walk! Deuteronomy 6 lays this out: "You must teach them [these commandments] to your children and talk about them when you are at home or out for a walk; at bedtime and the first thing in the morning. Tie them on your finger, wear them on your forehead, and write them on the doorposts of your house!" (Deut. 6:7–8, LB). This doesn't mean that I am to preach sermons at my children all day long! My conversation and teaching about Christ should grow naturally and constantly out of all that we do! And added to regular reading and memorizing of Scripture, we should fill our children's imaginations with the images of God's truth! For the past year one of my greatest fun times has been reading C. S. Lewis's *Narnia* chronicles to our ten-year-old at bedtime. He doesn't grasp all the symbolism now, and I don't try to explain it. But these images will help to open his mind to God's ways in an increasingly secularized, one-dimensional world.

Do I as a parent try to *isolate* my child from the evil influences of the world or to *immunize* him? Many Christian parents think their biggest job is to *protect* their children. I've got news for you: that may be the best way to *lose* them. We need to move from a defensive to an offensive posture, not so much to keep our children from losing their faith as to help them share it! Certainly there are blatantly evil influences from which I must protect them. But I also need to be aware that my children will be under these influences whether I like it or not, talk about these things with them, and prepare them to confront a world which lies in the evil one. According to Francis Schaeffer, some of the confused kids they get at L'Abri are from evangelical homes and churches where they've been told, "Don't ask questions; just believe." We must *encourage* our children to ask questions and as parents do the hard work of learning the answers, or learning where they can be found.

All of us need to grasp the significance of Blocher's third thesis: "The child is not already a responsible person: he *becomes* one." Children are not "small adults"; they can respond to the gospel only where they are in terms of responsibility. A young child may accept Christ with real meaning; I did at age five. But this childhood experience needs to be ratified at the age of "accountability" which varies with the individual—when a child begins to think of God as a Spirit, to understand sin as more than disobedience to parents, to be capable of personal decision and responsibility.

Real and lasting conversion of our offspring demands patience on the part of parent and pastor and responsibility on the part of children. If our evangelism is impatient, the fruit will be incomplete. We must nurture our children, not as a substitute for conversion, but as a preparation for it, carefully and prayerfully laying the logs on the fireplace and expecting God to ignite them at the right time.

Discouraged parents with rebellious youngsters should remember Monica, the mother of Augustine. She prostrated herself on the sands off the North Africa desert, weeping in prayer for her son's conversion, and could not understand how God could let him leave and go off to the fleshpots of pagan Rome. Little did she know that in Rome her son would hear Bishop Ambrose preach, be convicted of his sin, and find in God the end to his restless quest!

Evangelizing the Non-Christian Family

The strategy of "family evangelism" is growing rapidly today outside of North America. Veteran Korea missionary Roy Shearer reports that in Korean society, "The soundest way for a man to come to Christ is in the setting of his own family." The gospel, he notes, flows "along the web of family relationships." In India, Miss B. V. Subbamma, who has been so effective in evangelizing Hindus, believes that the Hindu family may be the only institution through which the gospel can be transmitted and received. Indonesia (along with many other nations) has witnessed tremendous "people movements" in which whole villages with all their families would turn to Christ. The Spirit of Jesus Church in Japan is growing rapidly through what they call "sweet potato vine" evangelism. They cultivate contacts with families—"the vine"—as opposed to individuals—"individual fruit."

Perhaps we in the West have been too culture bound! Perhaps we have been too individualistic! Perhaps our brothers and sisters in other parts of the world are leading us to rediscover a biblical pattern of family evangelism.

Isn't it true that one of the main results we hope for in evangelism is the healing of broken families? Then isn't it fair to ask whether the *strategy* of our evangelism aims at whole families? For example, we need *child* evangelism, *youth* evangelism, *adult* evangelism. But all of these should be seen in the context of *family* evangelism.

Communications specialists tell us that we must reach people at the point of "felt need" in their lives. Family concerns are often the "open filter" through which we can approach them with the good news of Christ. In the Billy Graham Crusades and my own Reachouts we've found that publicizing a family night with a message on the home usually brings the largest crowd and often the greatest response! Many uncommitted parents attend Bill Gothard's seminars and find Christ because they are seeking answers to family conflicts. Family crises—impending divorce, discipline problems, the death of a family member—often provide the divine "timing" which prepares hearts to respond.

We are always thrilled to hear stories like that of the couple who attended our Macon, Georgia, Reachout. That very week they were planning to file for divorce. They both came forward, he to receive Christ for the first time, she to rededicate her life. As they spoke with a pastor-counselor, the man poured out to his wife the wrongs he had done. She said, "In Christ's name I forgive you," and then shared with him the areas where she had wronged him. And this new Christian took her hands, looked her in the eyes, and said, "In Christ's name I forgive you." God gave them a new beginning!

Lost Valley Ranch, a guest ranch in Colorado, is one of the most effective family outreaches I have seen. Its founder and manager, Bob Foster, conceived the ranch as a means of contacting business and professional men at the point where they hurt most—their families. Lost Valley does not advertise itself as a "Christian" operation. Their ads in the *Wall Street Journal* and other papers emphasize only that they offer a wholesome family-oriented vacation. The program has no "religious" meetings outside a Sunday morning open-air worship service. They include separate activities for different ages but always have events that bring the families together. Before they've been there long, the guests sense something is different. There is a genuine love and personal concern on the part of the staff, all of whom are committed Christians. Even though there's no "happy hour," people are happy. At some of the evening western-style singing programs the staff will sing a hymn and explain what motivates the ranch. Guests start asking questions. Every week some open their lives to the God whose presence they have sensed. And for months to come others call back to say, "Bob, we're having a problem in our family. We know you're a devout man. Is there any way we can find the kind of relation with God you told us about?"

This family dimension needs to be included creatively in our various evangelistic outreaches. When you plan an evangelistic campaign in your city or church, how about including at least one meeting for the family, with the slogan, "No adult without bringing a child; no child unless accompanied by an adult!" The message could be "Believe on the Lord Jesus Christ and you shall be saved and your house," and the follow-up material would be designed to help the whole family start a new life with Christ.

When you have some effort for a special age group, why not tie in an outreach to other family members? Some months ago I gave a series of evangelistic addresses at the University of Maryland. One evening the student committee hosted a dinner to which they invited their parents, many of whom were non-Christians, and asked me to explain the purpose of the week to the parents, as a way of sharing the gospel with them too. Does your church or group plan something of this sort for parents, perhaps as part of a report or awards session at the end of a youth activity?

A number of churches are deliberately programing for the whole family. This has relevance, not only for Christian nurture, but also for evangelism! Not too many activities in our society are geared for whole families. Family camping or family worship services planned by our churches can have a tremendous appeal to parents seeking to pull their family together.

And what about the Christian school as an evangelistic agency? Is the Christian school a "cop-out" as some charge? Maybe, for some who seek primarily a haven where they can protect their children. But in Argentina the Christian Brethren are using schools as their main tool of outreach. Nonevangelical and even agnostic parents choose to send their children to these avowedly Christian schools because they are attracted by the strength of character and excellence of education which they see in them. The Brethren are doing some of their greatest reaping as a result of the Bible teaching and regular evangelistic services shared with these students and their families.

The Christian Home: Base for Evangelism

Among the first Christians one of the most important methods of spreading the gospel was by the use of homes. Those early believers met in the upper room of a house owned by John Mark's mother in Jerusalem (Acts 1:13, 12:12). Paul used Lydia's house and the jailer's at Philippi as evangelistic centers (Acts 16:15, 32–34). The Book of Acts shows us homes being used for informal evangelistic encounters, for meetings planned to hear the gospel, and for follow-up of inquirers.

Aquila and Priscilla have been held up as a model of husband-wife relationship in Christ. They were also first-rate evangelistic team! They knew how to use their home for worship, study, hospitality, and conversation to advance the gospel.

The example of the early Christians affected succeeding generations. Christians in Rome in the second and third centuries used the decorations in their homes as a witness to their fatih. Celsus, a bitter enemy of Christianity, sneered at the "stupid" housewives who gossiped Christianity at the laundry.

Those first Christians had few evangelistic tools, they had no radio or TV, no church buildings to mention, no printing presses, but they knew how to use their homes! Today an evangelistic breakthrough is taking place in the growing use of homes all over the world!

But the most important thing a Christian home can contribute to evangelism is its quality of life! God isn't calling us first to offer our homes as miniauditoriums for evangelistic meetings. The first thing he wants is for our homes to demonstrate transformed relationships!

A family where husband and wife love each other more deeply and faithfully as years go by, where a husband can affirm his wife's gifts without thinking he is giving up his manhood, where a wife cain joyfully adapt to her husband's leadership and still be liberated, where children are a gift and not a burden, where simplicity is the keynote and not slavery to consumerism, and where security in Christ is so real that children don't have to be rushed off to private school to flee integration is a powerful evangelistic statement before a word is said.

Have you ever noticed that while we find Jesus' Great Commission given in the Gospels and in the Book of Acts we don't find it repeated in the Epistles? Oh, we find Paul telling the Colossians to walk in wisdom "toward them that are without," but you don't find him telling them, "Go into all the world and preach the gospel." Why?

The first evangelists went throughout the world of their day preaching, making disciples, establishing Christian communities. In the cities where they went, they reached the "pool" of those who were prepared to understand and receive the gospel, namely, the Jews and the God-fearing Gentile proselytes. Then Paul and the other missionaries realized that, for the most part, the pagan world of their day was not prepared to hear and understand. First, they had to see the gospel lived out in daily relationships. Thus the emphasis in the Epistles is on being *in* Christ and living *out* Christ as husband and wife, parent and child, slave and master. Then, having seen the life of Christ fleshed out in living color, the pagans would ask, "How come?" and be ready to listen.

Discipleship in this area of family life must be high on the agenda for evangelism in our day. This doesn't mean we wait until our relationships are perfect before we share Christ with our neighbors. If we did, we'd never do it! No one's life or family is "good enough" to be a witness in itself. As an evangelist, when I'm preaching about how Jesus can change our family, I've also got to admit that I can still lose my temper on the tennis court (in a very spiritual way, of course!) and then snap at my wife for the next three hours! But this honest sharing of failure and how we learn to forgive each other can also be a powerful evangelistic word to the very human fellow-strugglers with whom we seek to share a realistic Christ!

Real family love is a radical statement today, and it will be even more so as society becomes more pagan. But the "saltiness" of Christian love has got to be exposed to have impact. Exposure demands that we build bridges of friendship to the world around. We've got to overcome the unbiblical idea that *separation* equals *isolation*. That's been one of the devil's major ploys in quarantining the contagious power of the gospel.

Remember how Jesus called Levi, that rascal of a tax collector? The first thing Levi did was to have a big party at his house, invite all of his gambling, drinking, rowdy friends, and ask Jesus to come as the guest of honor! "Worldliness!" we'd cry today. "Jesus, tell Levi to come out and be separate!" And so we'd close the door of Levi's house forever as an evangelistic outpost.

Obviously there's a balance called for, tension that every family has to work out on its own. We must be prepared to expose our family to non-Christians by inviting them in and by going where they are. But we can't *overexpose* our families, or we may lose what we're building. Time with the Lord and one another is just as important a priority as openness to non-Christians. But in the case of my own family, we feel God calling us to a much more radical obedience in opening our home to those who need our Savior.

How can we use our homes for evangelism? The first and most obvious way is through simple friendship, neighborly hospitality, inviting folks over for a meal. Sometimes the best witness is the unconscious witness of association. Home gatherings can provide the setting for natural, informal sharing of our faith.

A real estate developer in Dallas and his wife invite couples from their tennis club over for dinner and a chance to get better acquainted. Over coffee in the den he says something like this: "We don't have much chance to get acquainted on the tennis court. I thought you might like to get to know one another better. How about each of us sharing what we would most like the others to know about us?" He then begins, tells something of his background, and very simply explains that the priorities in his life are first, his walk with Jesus Christ, second, his family, and third, his business. The others then share what's most important to them, and, without pushing, the evening often results in follow-up conversations about Christ with someone who's been deeply moved.

We hear of many families who invite friends in to view the Billy Graham TV Crusades with them as an opener to sharing Christ.

Another approach is to invite neighbors in to meet some Christian—perhaps a visiting missionary or even a local friend—who knows how to turn the conversation to spiritual things and in an interesting, spontaneous way stimulate questions about Christ.

Others may want to take a more structured approach. Recently it was my privilege to speak at a dinner party for four hundred persons at a lovely home in Philadelphia. After a buffet supper in the garden I presented the claims of Christ to the assembled guests, all of whom knew what they were coming to hear! More than one hundred indicated they had received Christ that night in comment cards handed in. Christians who couldn't get their neighbors to church found they would attend such a meeting in the setting of a home. It was especially interesting to watch how a whole family, including some younger children, worked on the dinner party with an infectious enthusiasm—setting tables, welcoming guests, praying for God's blessing, and sorting through the comment cards afterward!

And what about inviting international students to share a meal or spend a holiday period in the home? I shall never forget the Taiwanese student in Canada who told me, "Something puzzled me about the Christian homes I visited in Canada. No matter how many members there were in the family, there was always one more! They were always talking to this unseen person, at meals and other times. And I could see the difference—the love—something I had not experienced in my home in Taiwan. I wanted what they had, and I found it was the Lord Jesus Christ. That's why I'm a Christian now!"

Christians should also use family occasions to communicate the gospel. Birthdays, weddings, and anniversaries are festive occasions to share with relatives and friends the joy of the Lord. And funerals can be a time to witness to the reality of his triumph even through the tears!

Another area of prime importance is ministry to singles and to the divorced. A church may often need to operate as an "extended family" to provide support and teaching and witness to those who don't have a full family of their own. Some congregations, like an Episcopal church in Texas, have helped form communities of young, single, working adults in apartments surrounding the church where they can live, study, play, share, and witness together.

Very little seems to have been written in this area. Parachurch groups, denominational evangelism departments, and Christian publishers should be encouraged to prepare materials to teach Christian families how God can use their homes as his evangelistic base. In Vancouver, British Columbia, our team is presently engaged in a two-year in-depth evangelism project. The training task force in Vancouver has prepared a seven-week study guide entitled "In the Spirit of Love." One of the exciting features is that the material is integrated for study at four levels—personal, small group, large group, and *in the family!* Parents are given suggestions, including games, to help the whole family see their opportunity to witness for Christ in the place God has put them.

THE FAMILY AND ITS MISSION

Remember Jesus' words about those who would *leave* home and father and mother for his sake and the gospel's? Our homes are not meant to be jealously guarded but to be lovingly offered in the service of Jesus and of our lost and lonely neighbors.

Nowhere is this more dramatically illustrated than in *The*

Hiding Place, the story of Corrie Ten Boom and her family. World Wide Pictures' screen version opened recently across North America. It vividly portrays this dedicated Dutch family who used a secret alcove in their home to hide Jewish refugees from the Nazis during World War II. Father Ten Boom and his daughters were confronted with an awful decision: Would they turn away their Jewish friends and guard their family's safety? Or would they risk their own family to protect others? With quiet courage they acknowledged that they could not confess Christ and turn away the Jews. Because God was their "hiding place," their home could be a "hiding place" for the wretched of the earth. And even though that decision led to arrest, concentration camps, and death, they did not *lose* their home in any final sense. What they did was to demonstrate that only as we share, only as we are willing to *lose* our homes for Jesus' sake, do we find them!

Study Guide

Gary Collins

The purpose of a study guide is to help individuals or groups of readers to better understand, evaluate, and interact with the ideas that are presented in a book or collection of articles. The chapters which comprise the preceding pages contain a number of insights and sometimes conflicting opinions, written by capable people who have given serious thought to the Christian family and how it can be strengthened. By adding a study guide, it is hoped that you will be encouraged to think back over what has been written and to arrive at some further conclusions of your own. Even more important, this study guide has been prepared to help you look at your own family so that you can make the changes which will build and develop family life in your house.

It is possible, of course, to work through this study guide on your own but you will find it more beneficial and interesting if you discuss these questions with your spouse, family members, and/or a group of people. The study guide has been designed, therefore, for individual study which leads to group interaction. Whenever you meet with a group, there should be a leader who can guide the discussion and stimulate interaction. The same leader can direct all of the discussions, or you may want to shift leadership responsibilities so that a different person, chosen from the group, leads each of the sessions.

Before a discussion, each person should read the chapter or chapters to be discussed, complete the first two assignments, and then look over the questions which follow. These questions are designed to facilitate discussion, encourage self-examination and stimulate people to make changes in their own attitudes and family life. In the discussions everyone should be encouraged to express his or her views, and the leader should try to keep the discussion from getting too far off the track. When there are irreconcilable differences within the group, the leader should have the right to stop discussion until more homework can be done, expert advice can be obtained, or the group agrees that discussion has reached a dead end.

One final comment: the questions and exercises which follow are merely suggestive. If you can think of questions which are better, use them. It might be more fun that way, and it might lead to greater changes within *your* family.

Chapter 1: Edith Schaeffer
What Is a Family?

1. In this chapter, Edith Schaeffer asks a question which is not easily answered: What is a family? How would you answer that question? Write down your definition.

2. Proverbs 31 is often viewed as a picture of the ideal wife or virtuous woman, but Schaeffer sees this passage as a guideline for the whole family. Read Proverbs 31. What does it say about the family in general? Does it say anything about Christian family life? Does it say anything about your family?

DISCUSSION QUESTIONS

3. If you are meeting in a group and have not done so already, introduce yourself to the other group members. Whether you are in a discussion group or considering these questions as a family, decide how you will proceed, how often you will meet, who will lead the discussions and what you hope to accomplish.

4. Now go back to question 1 above. What is a family? Share what you wrote down. Do you agree with Schaeffer's statement that "the *family* consists of a man and a woman who are married to each other and the children they have borne." Is this a "biblical definition" as Schaeffer maintains? What would you add or subtract from Schaeffer's definition? Give biblical support for your additions or subtractions.

5. Schaeffer gives nine descriptions of what a family is. What are these descriptions? (Each begins with the words, "a family is . . .") In each, ask the following questions: Do I agree with the author? Do I disagree? Why? What does the Bible say (if anything) about each of these nine statements?

6. Discuss your reactions to the following quotations from the chapter:

   a. There is . . . no complete democracy, and in the family there must be a "head" . . . this does not mean that there are men's jobs and women's jobs.
   b. When a child is two years old, he or she will demonstrate traits that portend the twenty-two year old.
   c. There are no perfect people, no perfect marriages, and no perfect relationships. Therefore, mothers and fathers and children need not feel guilty about not being the perfect or ideal family.
   d. Schools can help or hinder, and an informed parent can create a necessary balance in a child's home environment to counteract or support the school's influence. . . . The home should be the most educationally stimulating experience in a child's background.
   e. Fathers and mothers have been cruel to their children in neglecting to make truth known and in neglecting to make it exciting. . . . The excitement and the reality of all that the Bible teaches should be a normal part of discussion.

7. Schaeffer maintains that the family should be a living example of true spirituality. She suggests, for example, that as children trust and depend on parents they learn about trusting and depending on God; as they find shelter in the family, they learn about God's faithfulness; as they see how parents treat people, they learn about God's attitudes toward human beings. Do you agree with Schaeffer on these conclusions? Of what practical value is this to your family and to your church?

FOR FAMILY CONSIDERATION

8. Look over Schaeffer's nine descriptions of the family. Ask, How successful is our family in this task? What could we be doing differently? What are specific and practical steps that we can take to improve our family in each of these areas?

Chapter 2: Quentin Hyder
Developing Family Emotional Maturity

1. How would you evaluate your family? According to Quentin Hyder there is no such thing as a "normal" family, but there can be "ideal" families. Is your family ideal—as described in the last few paragraphs of this chapter? How could your family life be improved?

2. According to Hyder, love is "the essential ingredient which maintains communication and respect" in the home. Turn to the familiar 13th chapter of 1 Corinthians and read again about love. How can these verses apply to your marriage and family?

DISCUSSION QUESTIONS

3. Hyder lists principles for developing and maintaining stability in the home. What are these principles? Do you agree with each? Is each consistent with the Bible?

4. Discuss your reaction to the following quotations from Hyder's chapter:

   a. The emotional security of a loving home is the greatest single factor in obviating a child's need to search for satisfaction in superficial and ultimately disappointing relationships outside.
   b. Moral and religious principles should be taught primarily in the home, not at school, or even in church.
   c. The longer a child lives in a godly home the greater are his chances of embracing for himself a personal faith similar to that of his parents.
   d. It is the husband's responsibility to be the spiritual leader in the home.

5. What is the best way to deal with conflicts and disagreements in the home? Do you agree that thoughtlessness and selfishness are the two basic causes of marital disharmony? How do you react to Hyder's suggestions for conflict resolution under section 8A of his chapter?

6. Good communication is a basic requirement for family harmony. According to Hyder, good communication is not complete until three stages have been achieved. What are these? How could

these three stages be reached in practice? Is this a realistic guideline for improving communication in your family?

7. The author lists several principles for financial stability in the home. What are these? Are they workable principles?

FOR FAMILY CONSIDERATION

8. "A Christian home is significantly different from one in which Christ is not honored." In what ways does your home differ from those of your non-Christian neighbors? In what ways *should* your home be different? How can you make your home closer to the ideal about which Hyder writes? Does this chapter give you some practical suggestions? What practical steps do you plan to take in order to improve your home? When do you plan to start?

Chapter 3: Bruce Narramore
Christian Parenthood

1. It has been said that God takes amateurs in child rearing and makes them parents. If you are a mother or father, how could you improve in your effectiveness as a parent? Discuss this with your spouse. If you are not a parent, consider the question of how people like you could help others to become better parents.

2. In his chapter, Bruce Narramore cites Hebrews 12:3-11 and Matthew 7:9-11 as passages which point to a parallel between parenting and God's relationships with his children. Please read these passages. What do they teach you about Christian parenthood?

DISCUSSION QUESTIONS

3. How would you respond to the following question asked by Narramore in his chapter: "Does the Bible give us a realistic set of guidelines for raising children, and if so, what is it?"

4. "I would suggest that the Christian parent should *never* punish his or her child. We should discipline, but we should never punish." How do you respond to this suggestion? Before answering, be sure that you have read Narramore's discussion of this. Does the author have a biblical basis for his position?

5. Look at the quotation at the top of page 47. Do you agree with the quotation? If not, why not? Could you find biblical support for the author's position? Assuming that your view is different, can you find biblical support for your position?

6. The author is somewhat critical of seminars and books on child rearing which may be confusing and of questionable validity. What is your reaction to such materials? Look over Narramore's guidelines for evaluating such materials. What are the guidelines? Are they practical? Apply them to some books or seminar materials with which you are familiar.

7. In his paper, Narramore lists five specific suggestions for changing the quality of the Christian home. What are these suggestions (beginning at the top of page 41)? How, in a practical way, could they apply to your church?

FOR FAMILY CONSIDERATION

8. How can you be a better Christian parent in your family? Are there ways in which the children in your house could be more effectively trained and disciplined? Let everyone (parents and children alike) express their opinions about the parenting in your home. Try to arrive at some practical suggestions for improvement.

Chapter 4: Jay Kesler
Integrating Teenagers into the Family

1. What is your attitude toward teenagers? How do you get along with the teens in your house or in your church? How could you improve parent-teen relations in your home? What could *you* do to improve your church's ministry to teenagers?

2. The Bible doesn't say anything about teenagers specifically, but it does talk about young people. For example, see 1 Timothy 4:12, 2 Timothy 2:22, Titus 2:6-8, Proverbs 20:29, 1 Peter 5:5. Do these and similar Scripture verses have any bearing on the integrating of teenagers into the family?

DISCUSSION QUESTIONS

3. "Young people will naturally gravitate toward a certain family climate. In the creation of this climate . . . healthy relationships will develop." How is such a climate created in the home? Does your home have such a climate? Is your home or church like these of the runaways who complained: "They quit listening to me"?

4. Jay Kesler, busy president of a national teen-age organization, describes in this chapter how he dealt with his own daughter's decision to read a novel of questionable moral and literary quality. What did Kesler do? Was this a wise choice? Why (or why not)? What are other ways in which an "open attitude" can be developed in the home?

5. In his chapter, Kesler describes a research study in which students in school tend to perform exactly as their teachers expect them to perform. Is it possible that when we expect teens to be problems they become problems? What are the implications of this for family life?

6. How do you respond to the following quotations from Kesler's chapter? Try to think of practical ways in which these quotations could apply to your home or your church:

   a. A young person who is pampered, overprotected, or untrusted, even for good motives like Christian parental love, will disengage from the family stream to try his or her wings.

   b. When asked why they hang around certain people or places, almost invariably teens will say, "They respect me, they accept me for myself, I feel comfortable here." A family is a place where members should feel comfortable. Teens can sense rejection of themselves, their friends, their music, dress, ideas. Some people who are unable to separate the person from his habits, ideas, clothing, and so on, thus unknowingly drive youth away or to silence or estrangement within the home.

7. Read over Kesler's ten suggestions for creating a home in which young people feel affirmed, loved, and trusted. How would you evaluate each of these suggestions?

FOR FAMILY CONSIDERATION

8. In the privacy of your own home, go over Kesler's ten suggestions again, discussing each as a family. How could each be ap-

plied to your family? Are Kesler's suggestions realistic for you? How could they be adapted to improve family–teen relationships in your house?

Chapter 5: Waldo J. Werning
Family Financial Planning

1. How do you spend your money? It has been suggested that one good way to learn about a family's values is to look into the family checkbook. According to Waldo Werning, "economic decisions are made on the basis of one's philosophy of life. . . . Attitudes and spiritual values . . . determine how money is spent—for good or evil." Are you happy with the way you budget and spend your money? Do you suppose God is happy about your management of money? How could you spend your money more wisely?

2. Read Matthew 6:19–33, 1 Timothy 3:3, 6:6–10. From these Scripture verses, what can you learn about the ways in which Christians should handle their finances? What do these verses teach about our attitudes toward money?

DISCUSSION QUESTIONS

3. According to Werning, "values based on scriptural standards should mold our spending patterns." What are some scriptural standards which can guide our values and use of money? Does your answer to question 2, above, help here?

4. Discuss the following quotations from Werning's chapter—do you agree or disagree? Why? In what ways do each of these apply to you?

   a. As Christians we have three objectives in spending our money: God's glory, our own needs, and the needs of others.
   b. Getting more money is not always the solution to financial solvency.
   c. Churches have a special opportunity and obligation to provide guidance to their members in money management.
   d. [According to Haggai's prophecy] people experienced inflation and money problems because they put their own affairs and homes before God and his work.

5. Near the top of page 69, Werning gives five rules for credit buying. Do you agree? When is credit buying wrong for the Christian?

6. Children should be taught how to manage money. How can this be done? To what extent do you agree with Werning's suggestions on children's stewardship?

7. In what practical ways can your church help families with their financial planning and money management? Are the ten principles on page 67 suggestive of a place to begin?

FOR FAMILY CONSIDERATION

8. According to Werning, family members should talk together about how they have spent money in the past and how they should budget for the future. Has your family had such conversations? How can your family finances be discussed and handled more effectively in the future? On pages 72 and 73, Werning lists a number of practical principles for family finance. Discuss these as a family.

Chapter 6: William D. Gwinn
Leisure, Vacations, and the Family

1. Reread the first four paragraphs of this chapter. To what extent does this describe your family? How could your family improve? Would vacations help?

2. According to Gwinn, Jesus and his disciples took vacations. Do you think there is biblical support for such a statement? Are Mark 1:35 and Luke 9:10 referring to mini-vacations?

DISCUSSION QUESTIONS

3. In his chapter, Gwinn assumes that family vacations are both good and necessary. List some advantages and disadvantages of family vacations. Which list is longer? What does this say about family vacationing? Do you feel guilty about taking time off? Why?

4. Discuss the following quotations from Gwinn's chapter. Indicate whether you agree or disagree and give reasons for your opinion.

a. As urgent as is the need to make Christ known, there is no justification for "workaholics" in the kingdom of God. . . . "Burning the candle at both ends" is not a wise or disciplined spiritual exercise.

b. Hobbies and diversions which are strictly solitary in nature can tend to erode family unity to a major degree. They need to be shared in some way.

c. There is a crucial need for concentrated periods of time when families can get away from the usual routine and enjoy new places, new people, and new experiences.

d. "The family who prays together stays together."

e. As valuable as programs of visitation have been, the Bible has far more to say about the ministry of hospitality, than it does about visitation, other than of the widowed, elderly, and afflicted.

5. Gwinn is critical of local church programs which, with a variety of programs and meetings for individuals, split the family. What can the church do to build family unity? Can a family camping program, such as Gwinn describes, build families in your church?

FOR FAMILY CONSIDERATION

6. What is the attitude of your family toward vacations? Do you take vacations regularly? If not, why not? How could your family improve your leisure time together? What are some practical things you can do in the very near future to improve leisure and vacations in your family?

Chapter 7: Mark Hatfield
The Family in Today's World

1. What are the outside pressures which influence your family? What have you tried to do about them? What family pressures do you especially need to work on? How are you planning to do this?

2. In his chapter, Senator Mark Hatfield writes about the healing influence of love. What do the following passages say to you about love and your family: 1 John 4:7, 16, 18–21; Ephesians 5:25, 28, 33, 6:4; Titus 2:2–5?

DISCUSSION QUESTIONS

3. In the middle of page 90, Hatfield lists three assumptions about the family. What are these? Do you agree? Why (or why not)?

4. According to Hatfield, "the body of Christ is an extended family. The smaller family units within the body both support the larger body and are supported by it." What does this have to do with the relationship between your church and your family? Would Edith Schaeffer agree with Senator Hatfield that the church actually is an extended family? (See page 11.) What is your opinion? Why?

5. Hatfield quotes Uri Brofenbrenner's view that there are social forces in our society which create loneliness and "the loss of a sense of community." Can and should the government do anything to change social forces which threaten the family? If we leave this problem for the government to solve, are we forsaking our responsibility as individual Christian family members?

6. "The church of Jesus Christ today has a unique opportunity to offer society a constructive alternative to present trends of family erosion." What can the church do that is practical and feasible?

7. The author writes, "I believe that it is not the institution of the family that has failed. It is rather the individuals who have failed to practice love and discipline." How can you, as an individual, practice love and discipline? What would this do for your family and/or the families in your church and community?

FOR FAMILY CONSIDERATION

8. Reread the first paragraph of Hatfield's chapter. Could something like this happen to your family? What can you do together and individually to prevent the erosion of your family life, while at the same time allowing family members to develop and express each one's uniqueness and individuality?

Chapter 8: Ted Ward
The Christian's Family in Society

1. In his thought-provoking chapter, Ted Ward describes a number of ways in which society influences families and families influence

society. Think about your family. In what ways (good and bad) is it influenced by society or having an influence on society? Are you happy about this?

2. Read Romans 13. What does this passage say about the Christian's response to society? Does this have any relevance for families in America today—including your family?

DISCUSSION QUESTIONS

3. On pages 98–99, Ward lists three conclusions about the family. What are these? Do you agree? How can the Christian family become "distinctly different from the secular family"?

4. According to Ward, Christians who are "salt in the general society," must at times fight secular society on some issues. Is this biblical? In what ways and on what issues should we be fighting for families in our culture?

5. Beginning on page 100, Ward identifies several social influences that are eroding the family. What are these influences? Do you agree that these are eroding influences? What would you add to Ward's list? Give special consideration to the author's comments about television and about the public school.

6. For each of the following (a) define in your own words what is meant, (b) discuss Ward's solution to the problem and (c) consider how churches can help families face these issues: *materialism, competitive greed and self-centered individualism, faulty communication, relativism and deterioration of justice.*

FOR FAMILY CONSIDERATION

7. Without withdrawing from society, how can your family prevent the erosions which Ward describes? Be practical and specific. Give some special thought to family policies of TV viewing and the teaching of values.

Chapter 9: Basil Jackson
Drugs, Adolescence, and the Family

1. In this chapter, Basil Jackson raises an important issue for Christian families—how we teach values. What values are being taught

and demonstrated in your family? What, for example, are your family values concerning honesty, church attendance, moral purity, money, etc.? Are you satisfied with these values? How could you change?

2. In this chapter, Jackson discusses the ways in which one's conscience is developed. Look up the following Scripture verses dealing with the conscience. Acts 24:16; Romans 2:15; 1 Corinthians 8:7; 1 Timothy 3:8-11; Hebrews 9:14; 1 Peter 3:16. These verses are not directed toward the family, but do they say anything about conscience development in Christian children?

DISCUSSION QUESTIONS

3. Near the beginning of his chapter Jackson cites some things which can have a "disintegrating effect" on the family. These influences include advertising in the news media, the increasing numbers of nonproductive people in the family, automation, spectator sports, the influence of psychological theories which advocate permissiveness in child rearing, and the sexual revolution. How does each of these contribute to family disintegration? What can be done *by you* to prevent these influences from adversely affecting your family and the families in your community or church?

4. How can and should values be taught in the home?

5. According to Jackson, there are two major tasks of adolescence. What are these? What does this have to do with values and/or drug use among teenagers?

6. Jackson lists five reasons why adolescents commonly turn to drug use. What are these reasons? In what ways can the home and church counteract these influences?

7. Discuss your reaction to the following quotations:

   a. Tranquilizers are medical compounds which affect certain areas of the brain and blot out pain, anxiety, and the pressure of having to think. This is very similar to the effect of much that appears currently in the world of music and entertainment.

   b. [According to David Cooper] the bourgeois nuclear family unit, rather than being the matrix for interpersonal contact and communication, has become the ultimate place of non-meeting. This is, of course, the exact opposite of the divine institution and God's plan.

c. If value systems developed within the family have not demonstrated that some things are more important than peer group acceptance and popularity, then resort to drugs may be accepted as the price of initiation.

d. It should not surprise us . . . that the adolescent should use a variety of pills or alcohol to treat . . . anxiety when, in effect, although perhaps legally, his or her parents may be doing exactly the same thing.

FOR FAMILY CONSIDERATION

8. According to the author of this chapter, "the production of a stable family unit requires the expenditure of energy—it requires work. . . . Without such work, family and personal cohesion is gradually eroded." What are you as a family doing to *work* on your relationships? Are values being taught in your family? What are these values? How could your family work together to do a better job of learning values?

Chapter 10: C. Markham Berry
The Family and Mental Illness

1. What would be the effect on your present family if you had a seriously ill, aged, or mentally disturbed person in the home? Would there be advantages as well as disadvantages?

2. What is your attitude toward the chronically ill? Are you sympathetic? Repulsed? Tolerant? Eager to help? As Christians, what should be our attitude toward the sick? The following Bible verses might help with your answer: Matthew 25:31–40; Luke 10:30–37.

DISCUSSION QUESTIONS

3. In your group discuss your answers to questions 1 and 2 above.

4. How are (a) the physically ill (b) the retarded (c) the disabled (d) the mentally ill and (e) the aged cared for in your community? Suppose some of these people were taken into homes. How would this affect (a) the homes (b) your church?

5. In what ways can your church minister to families which have a sick or disabled person at home? How can the church minister to the patient? Be specific. Is your church ministering effectively to such patients and families? If not, why not?

6. According to Markham Berry, it's important to keep lines of communication open within the family when an ill person is living in the home. How can a family maintain this good communication?

FOR FAMILY CONSIDERATION

7. Has your family ever considered taking in a sick or disabled person? What would be the advantages and disadvantages? Is it something you should do? What might be God's will for your family on this issue?

Chapter 11: Matthew S. Prince
Friendship Evangelism

1. In the first ten chapters, this book has emphasized ways in which we can build stronger relationships within families and resist disruptive pressures from outside the home. In the two final chapters, the emphasis shifts to a consideration of how the home can become a channel of Christian outreach to the communities in which we live. To what extent is your family reaching out to others? Could you be having a better, more effective outreach? How?

2. Reread the Great Commission (Matthew 28:18–20). How did Jesus use homes to proclaim the gospel? See, for example, Mark 2:1–12 and John 12:1–11.

DISCUSSION QUESTIONS

3. Discuss your reaction to the following quotations from the chapter by Matthew Prince:

   a. If we are concerned only with our well-being as a family unit and never reach beyond ourselves, then we are not following the heart of Jesus Christ.

   b. In contemporary religion, we have become so meeting conscious, crowd conscious, and technique conscious that we are in danger of overlooking the strategic value of the home in carrying out the Great Commission. In the biblical pattern of reaching others for Christ, the home plays a significant role.

c. The home may offer more potential for showing the love of Christ than any vehicle available to us.

d. The home that is involved in the Great Commission will experience Christ's kind of fulfilling joy.

4. According to Prince, "having a balanced, healthy, harmonious Christian home is one of the best things that can be accomplished in life, but it is not the top priority item. The Great Commission is." What are the advantages and disadvantages of using the home as a basis for "friendship evangelism"?

5. If it is true, as Prince suggests, that many people are hostile toward religious buildings and religious meetings, how can the church be involved in evangelism through the home? Can and should the church be an evangelistic training center for families? How could this training be done? In what ways could this change the current programs and ministry of your church?

FOR FAMILY DISCUSSION

6. What could your family be doing as a family, in reaching out to others for Christ? Is friendship evangelism a realistic possibility for your family? How could you get started? When do you plan to begin?

Chapter 12: Leighton Ford
The Family—Foundation for Evangelism

1. According to Leighton Ford, "non-Christian families are often unreached because Christian families have the blahs!" Does your family have the blahs? How can you have a more dynamic family relationship?

2. Aquila and Priscilla are described in this chapter as a "model of husband-wife relationship in Christ" and a "first-rate evangelistic team" who "knew how to use their home for worship, study, hospitality, and conversation to advance the gospel." Read Acts 18:2,

3, 18, 26; Romans 16:3–5; and 1 Corinthians 16:19. Can this husband and wife provide a model for your family outreach?

DISCUSSION QUESTIONS

3. On page 145, Ford outlines a strategy of family evangelism. Re-
state this strategy in your own words. How could such a strategy
be used by your family and the families in your church?

4. "Do you realize how crucial it is that my wife and I model the
gospel in our relationships in the home? Children learn through
watching the behavior of their parents. . . . Discipleship . . . is
not a communicator of knowledge, but a communication of life."
What kind of a Christian model exists in your home? Do the
children in your home see evangelism and discipleship as an important part of the family priorities? How can this be improved
in your house? Is development in this area a necessary first step
which comes before your family reaches out to others?

5. In his chapter, Ford makes a number of challenging statements.
What is your reaction to each of the following? How, in a practical way, could each of the following be applied to you, your
family, and for your church's ministry?

   a. Do I as a parent try to *isolate* my child from the evil influences
   of the world or to immunize him? Many Christian parents think
   their biggest job is to *protect* their children. I've got news for
   you: that may be the best way to *lose* them.

   b. According to Edith Schaeffer, some of the confused kids they
   get at L'Abri are from evangelical homes and churches where
   they've been told, "Don't ask questions; just believe." We must
   encourage our children to ask questions and as parents do the
   hard work of learning the answers.

   c. The most important thing a Christian home can contribute to
   evangelism is its quality of life! God isn't calling us first to
   offer our homes as mini-auditoriums for evangelistic meetings.
   The first thing he wants is for our homes to demonstrate transformed relationships!

   d. We've got to overcome the unbiblical idea that *separation*
   equals *isolation*. That's been one of the devil's major ploys in
   quarantining the contagious power of the gospel.

   e. Our homes are not meant to be jealously guarded but to be
   lovingly offered in the service of Jesus and of our lost and
   lonely neighbors.

6. In the middle of page 149, Ford suggests that in the church we should be thinking seriously about "family evangelism." What would this involve? How could family evangelism be initiated through your church?

FOR FAMILY DISCUSSION

7. In this chapter the author asks, "How can we use our home for evangelism?" Answer this question as it applies to *your* home. In addition to evangelism, are there other ways in which you can touch lives for Christ through your home and family?

8. What has this book taught you about living and growing together as a family? In what ways will your family change as a result of reading and discussing this book? Have you started making the changes?